SCOTTISH CERTIFICATE OF EDUC

Credit
PHYSICS

The Scottish Certificate of Education Examination Papers
are reprinted by special permission of
THE SCOTTISH QUALIFICATIONS AUTHORITY

ISBN 0 7169 9276 0
© *Robert Gibson & Sons, Glasgow, Ltd., 1998*

The answers to the questions do not emanate from the Authority

ROBERT GIBSON · Publisher
17 Fitzroy Place, Glasgow, G3 7SF.

SCOTTISH CERTIFICATE OF EDUCATION

Time: 1 hour 45 minutes

PHYSICS
STANDARD GRADE
Credit Level

INSTRUCTIONS TO CANDIDATES

1. All questions should be attempted.
2. The questions may be answered in any order but all answers are to be written clearly and legibly in ink.
3. Write your answers where indicated by the question or in the space provided after the question.
4. If you change your mind about answer you may score it out and rewrite it in the space provided at the end of the answer book.
5. Before leaving the examination room this book must be given to the Invigilator. If you do not, you may lose all the marks for this paper.
6. Any necessary data will be found in the **Data Sheet**.

CONTENTS

1994 Credit Physics	4
1995 Credit Physics	26
1996 Credit Physics	49
1997 Credit Physics	71
1998 Credit Physics	95
Answers	119

COPYING PROHIBITED

Note: This publication is **NOT** licensed for copying under the Copyright Licensing Agency's Scheme, to which Robert Gibson & Sons are not party.

All rights reserved. No part of this publication may be reproduced; stored in a retrieval system; or transmitted in any form or by any means — electronic, mechanical, photocopying, or otherwise — without prior permission of the publisher Robert Gibson & Sons, Ltd., 17 Fitzroy Place, Glasgow, G3 7SF.

DATA SHEET

Speed of light in materials

Material	Speed in m/s
Air	3.0×10^8
Carbon dioxide	3.0×10^8
Diamond	1.2×10^8
Glass	2.0×10^8
Glycerol	2.1×10^8
Water	2.3×10^8

Speed of sound in materials

Material	Speed in m/s
Aluminium	5200
Air	340
Bone	4100
Carbon dioxide	270
Glycerol	1900
Muscle	1600
Steel	5200
Tissue	1500
Water	1500

Gravitational field strengths

	Gravitational field strength on the surface in N/kg
Earth	10
Jupiter	26
Mars	4
Mercury	4
Moon	1.6
Neptune	12
Saturn	11
Sun	270
Venus	9

Specific heat capacity of materials

Material	Specific heat capacity in J/kg °C
Alcohol	2350
Aluminium	902
Copper	386
Glass	500
Glycerol	2400
Ice	2100
Lead	128
Silica	1033
Water	4180

Specific latent heat of fusion of materials

Material	Specific latent heat of fusion in J/kg
Alcohol	0.99×10^5
Aluminium	3.95×10^5
Carbon dioxide	1.80×10^5
Copper	2.05×10^5
Glycerol	1.81×10^5
Lead	0.25×10^5
Water	3.34×10^5

Melting and boiling points of materials

Material	Melting point in °C	Boiling point in °C
Alcohol	−98	65
Aluminium	660	2470
Copper	1077	2567
Glycerol	18	290
Lead	328	1737
Turpentine	−10	156

Specific latent heat of vaporisation of materials

Material	Specific latent heat of vaporisation in J/kg
Alcohol	11.2×10^5
Carbon dioxide	3.77×10^5
Glycerol	8.30×10^5
Turpentine	2.90×10^5
Water	22.6×10^5

SI Prefixes and Multiplication Factors

Prefix	Symbol	Factor	
giga	G	1 000 000 000	$= 10^9$
mega	M	1 000 000	$= 10^6$
kilo	k	1000	$= 10^3$
milli	m	0.001	$= 10^{-3}$
micro	μ	0.000 001	$= 10^{-6}$
nano	n	0.000 000 001	$= 10^{-9}$

SCOTTISH CERTIFICATE OF EDUCATION
1994

FRIDAY, 13 MAY
1.30 PM – 3.15 PM

PHYSICS
STANDARD GRADE
Credit Level

1. The table below gives information about the wavelength and output power of some types of laser.

Type of laser	Wavelength m	Output power W
Excimer	3.2×10^{-7}	20.0
Argon	4.9×10^{-7}	2.0
Dye	5.5×10^{-7}	0.5
Helium-neon	6.3×10^{-7}	0.005
Nd-YAG	10.6×10^{-7}	50.0

The visible spectrum has wavelengths ranging from 4.0×10^{-7} m to 7.0×10^{-7} m.

(a) Which laser emits infrared radiation?

....

(b) Name **one** medical use of infrared radiation.

....

(c) Calculate the frequency of light from the helium-neon laser.

Space for working and answer

(d) Light from an argon laser is used to treat a patient's eye. During the treatment, the laser fires 15 short pulses of light. Each pulse lasts 0.2 second.

Calculate the energy given out by the laser during the treatment.

Space for working and answer

2. Videophones are special telephones which can be used to send both pictures (video) and sound between Glasgow and London.

GLASGOW   LONDON

The video signals of the videophone are produced by a small television camera.

(*a*) When a videophone is used, the video signal is combined with a carrier wave to produce a modulated signal. Diagrams representing the video signal and the carrier wave are shown below.

Draw the modulated signal in the space provided.

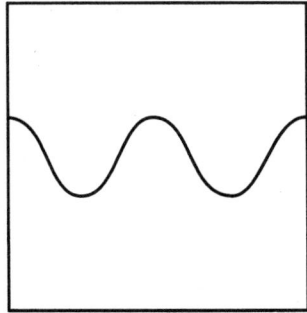
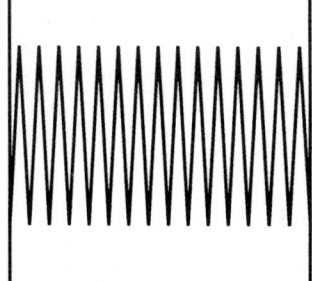
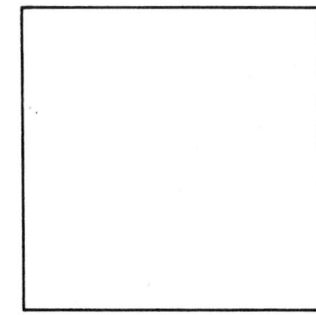

video signal   carrier wave   modulated signal

(*b*) A modulated signal from a videophone in Glasgow is converted into a light signal at a telephone exchange in Glasgow. This light signal is transmitted along a glass optical fibre to a telephone exchange in London. The length of the optical fibre is 700 km.

Calculate the time taken for the light signal to travel from Glasgow to London.

Space for working and answer

(c) A videophone picture received in London may be displayed on a large black and white television screen.

Describe, with the aid of a diagram, how the picture is built up on the television screen.

Space for diagram and answer

....
....
....
....
....
....
....

3. The heating elements of one make of toaster are connected as shown in figure 1. Figure 2 shows how the heating elements are arranged in a second make of toaster. The resistances of the heating elements are as indicated in the figures.

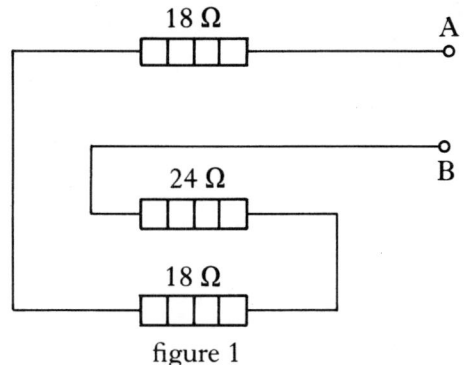

figure 1

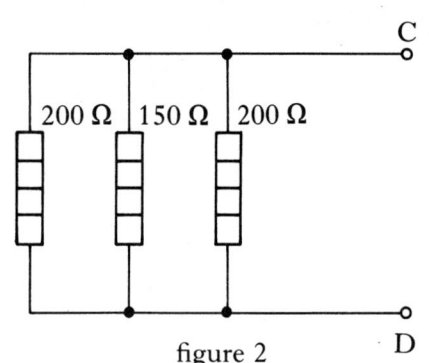

figure 2

(a) Calculate the resistance between points A and B in figure 1.

Space for working and answer

(b) Calculate the resistance between points C and D in figure 2.

Space for working and answer

(c) Calculate the power of the toaster shown in figure 2 when the 240 V mains supply is connected to C and D.

Space for working and answer

(d) One of the heating elements shown in **figure 1** burns out and the toaster stops working. This fault cannot be seen.

An electrician tries to identify which heating element is faulty. She disconnects the toaster from the mains supply and uses a multimeter which can be set to measure either **current** or **voltage** or **resistance.**

She connects the multimeter across each element in turn.

(i) What quantity should the multimeter be set to measure?

....

(ii) How does the electrician use the multimeter readings to identify the faulty element?

....

....

....

(iii) The multimeter will indicate either an open or a short circuit when connected across the faulty element.

Which fault will it indicate in this case?

....

4. A radioactive element emits gamma radiation. The graph below shows how the activity of the element decreases with time.

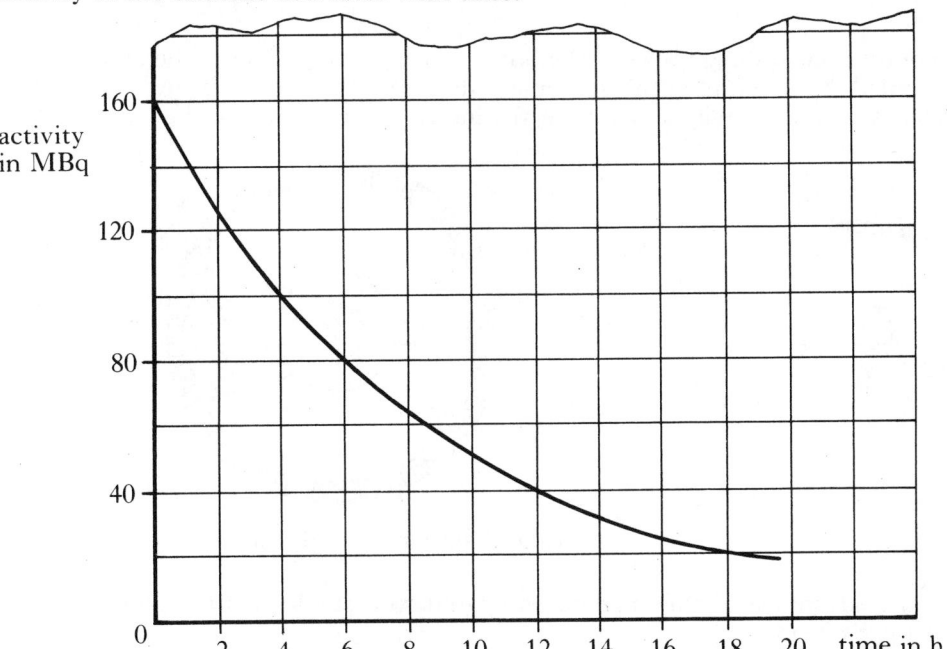

(a) What is the half-life of the radioactive element?

Space for working and answer

(b) As part of a medical examination, a patient has to drink a solution containing a sample of this radioactive element. The examination involves detecting the radiation coming from the radioactive element inside the patient's body.

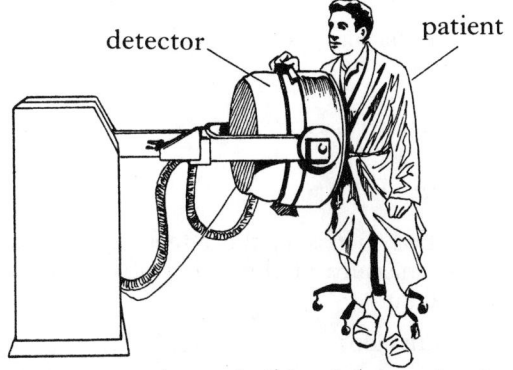

Explain why a gamma source is needed for the examination.

....

....

(c) A computerised tomography (CT) scanner has a moving X-ray tube and is surrounded by a number of stationary detectors as shown below. The scanner is used to display a picture of the inside of a patient's head.

State the advantage of this method compared to a single X-ray picture of the patient's head.

....

.... 1

(d) A small brain tumour can be treated using a chemical which emits alpha radiation. The chemical is absorbed by the tumour. The alpha radiation produces ionisation which destroys the tumour.

(i) What is meant by ionisation?

....

....

....

.... 2

(ii) Suggest why alpha radiation is used for this treatment rather than beta or gamma radiation.

....

.... 1

(e) When radiation is absorbed in tissue, the effect depends on the tissue and the type of radiation. A measure of the effect of the radiation on tissue is given by the dose equivalent.

State the unit of dose equivalent.

.... 1

5. When money is inserted into a drinks machine, a drink may be obtained and change given if necessary. The machine contains three coin chutes to enable it to give change. When the machine is able to give change, a light emitting diode (LED), at eye level, glows steadily. If the machine is unable to give change, the LED flashes on and off continuously to warn the customer.

Figure 1 shows part of the circuit which controls the operation of the LED.

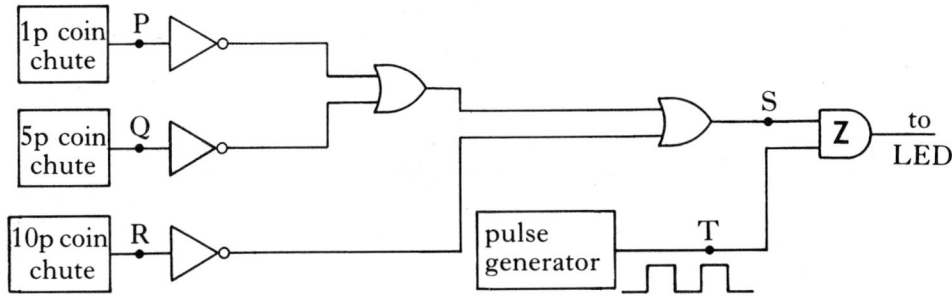

figure 1

The electronic outputs from the coin chutes are labelled P, Q and R.

When there are no coins in a chute, then its output is at logic level 0.

When there are coins in a chute, then its output is at logic level 1.

(a) A table may be constructed to show the logic levels at P, Q, R and S shown in figure 1. Part of the table is shown below.

Complete the table to show the logic levels at P, Q, R and S for the two rows shown.

P	Q	R	S
0	1	1	
			0

(b) The pulse generator produces an output at T in figure 1. This output is shown in figure 2.

figure 2

What happens to the logic output of gate Z when the logic level at S is 1?

Explain your answer.

....

....

....

....

(c) An LED is connected to the output of gate Z as shown in figure 3.

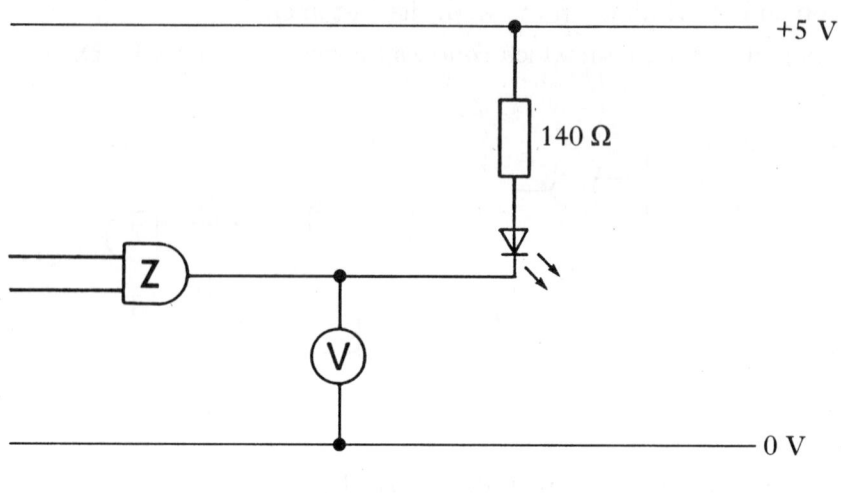

figure 3

When the output from gate Z is at logic level 0, the voltmeter reads 0 volt.
When the output from gate Z is at logic level 1, the voltmeter reads 5 volts.

(i) What is the logic level of the output from gate Z when the LED is lit?

....

(ii) When lit, the current in the LED is 20 mA.
Calculate the voltage across the LED.

Space for working and answer

6. A pupil sets up the apparatus shown below in an experiment to calculate a value for the specific latent heat of vaporisation of water.

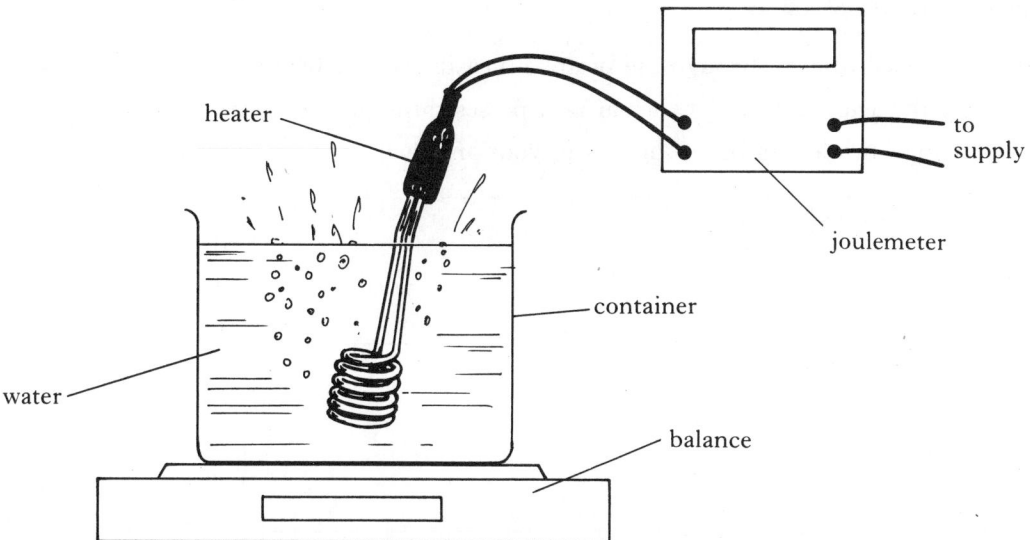

The reading on the balance remains steady as the water is brought to the boil.

The pupil then observes that the reading on the balance gradually decreases.

The energy supplied during the time taken for the reading on the balance to drop by 0·15 kg is measured by the pupil to be $3·15 \times 10^5$ J.

(a) Calculate a value for the specific latent heat of vaporisation of water from the pupil's experiment.

Space for working and answer

(b) During the experiment, the pupil noticed that water splashes out of the container due to the vigorous boiling.

(i) Explain why the splashing is likely to cause a lower value than expected for the specific latent heat of vaporisation of water.

....

....

....

....

(ii) How could this splashing be reduced?

....

....

7. A car is travelling along a straight road. An electronic timer is used to time how long the car takes to pass through an infrared beam. The car has a mass of 1100 kg and a length of 4·5 m.

(a) The time taken to pass through the beam is measured to be 0·34 s.

Calculate the average speed of the car as it passes through the beam.

(Use an appropriate number of figures in your answer.)

Space for working and answer

(b) A graph of the car's speed against time is shown in figure 1.

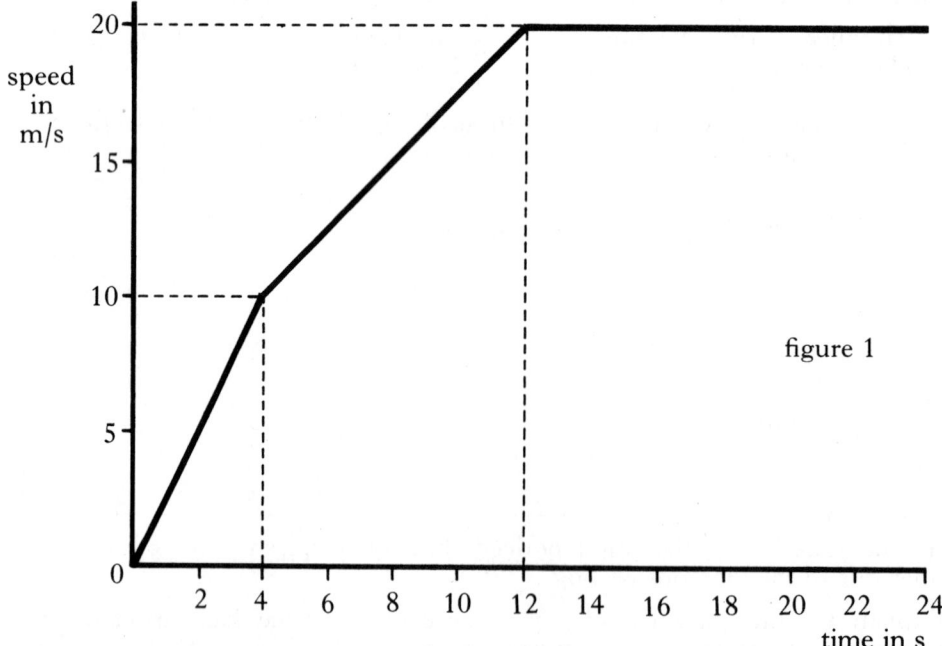

figure 1

Calculate the unbalanced force on the car between 4 s and 12 s.

Space for working and answer

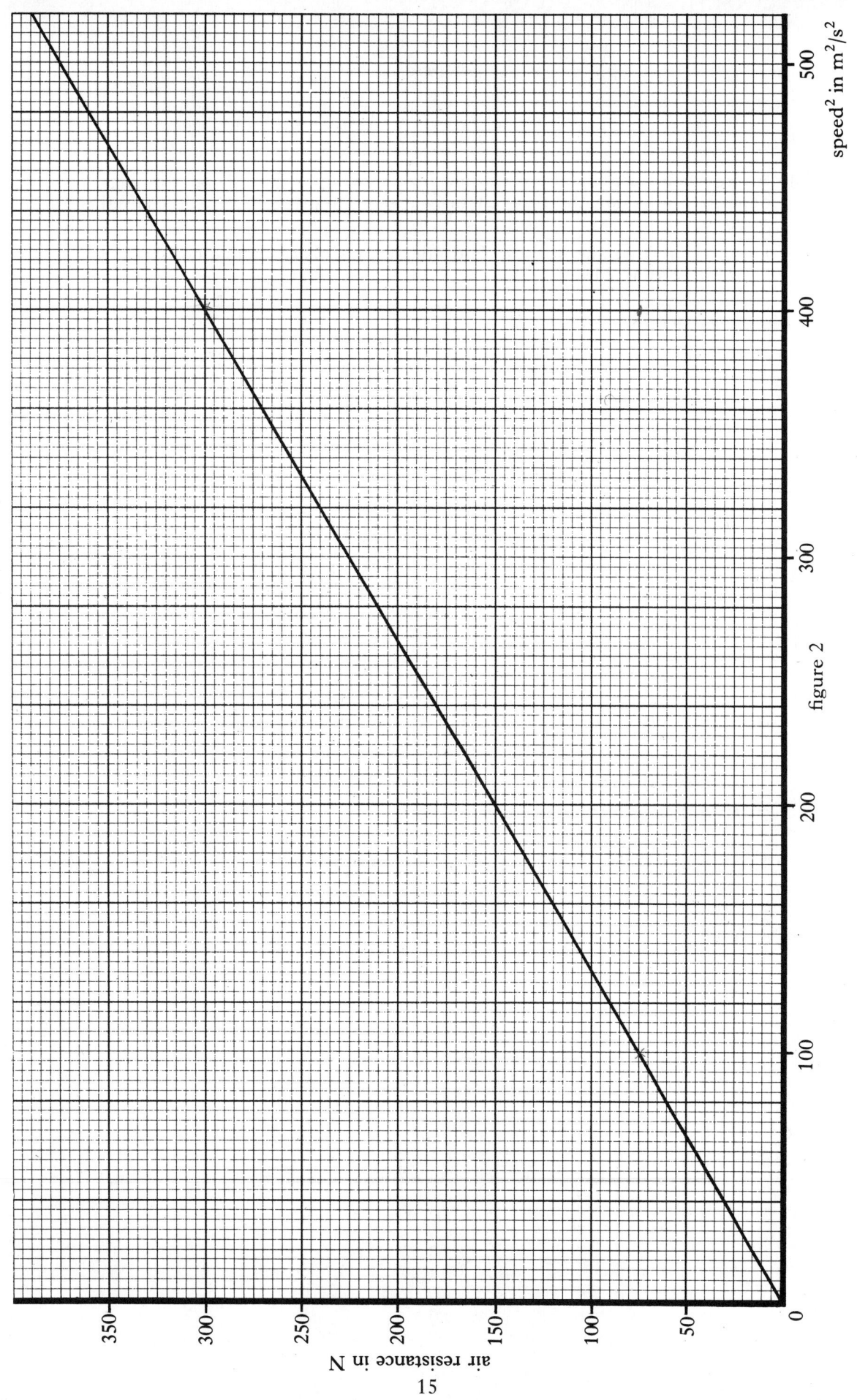
figure 2

(c) Air resistance acts on the car while it is moving. Figure 2, on the page opposite, shows how the air resistance varies when plotted against the speed squared.

Using data from the graphs, find the air resistance acting on the car between 12 s and 20 s.

Space for working and answer

(d) The car's average fuel consumption increases when a very light unladen roof rack is placed on the car. Explain why this happens.

....

....

8. (*a*) A 25 kΩ resistor is connected in series with a thermistor and a 12 V supply as shown in figure 1.

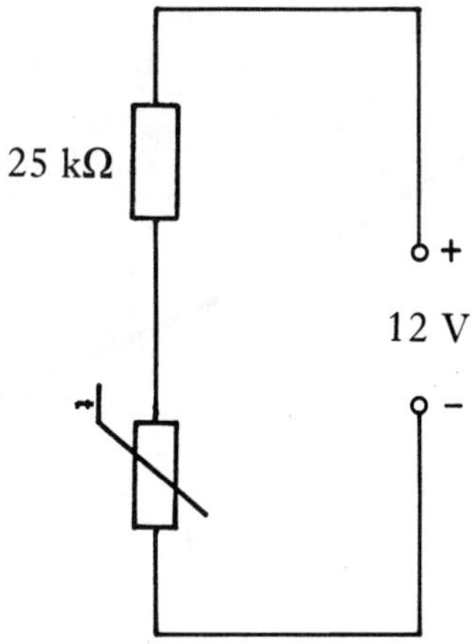

figure 1

At a particular temperature the voltage across the thermistor is 2 V.

(i) Calculate the voltage across the resistor.

Space for working and answer

(ii) Calculate the resistance of the thermistor.

Space for working and answer

(b) A graph of resistance of the thermistor against temperature is shown in figure 2.

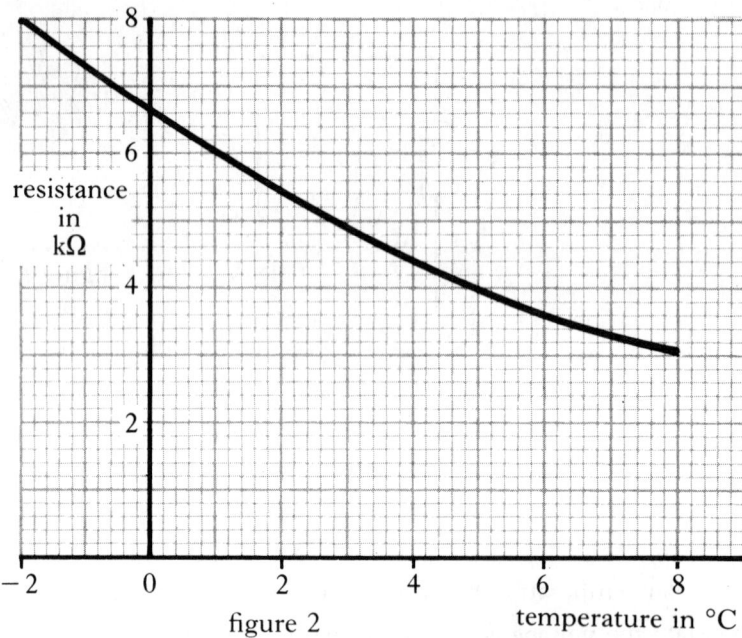

figure 2

Use the graph to estimate the temperature of the thermistor.

....

(c) Some cars are fitted with a warning device as shown in figure 3. The circuit alerts the driver when there is a risk of ice on the road.

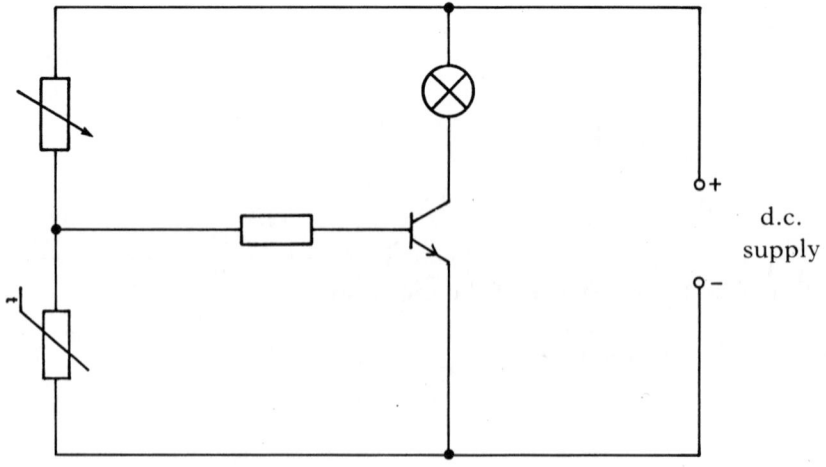

figure 3

Describe how the circuit works.

....

....

....

....

9. The diagram shows a water chute at a leisure pool. The top of the chute is 11·25 m above the edge of the pool. A girl, of mass 50 kg, climbs from the edge of the pool to the top of the water chute.

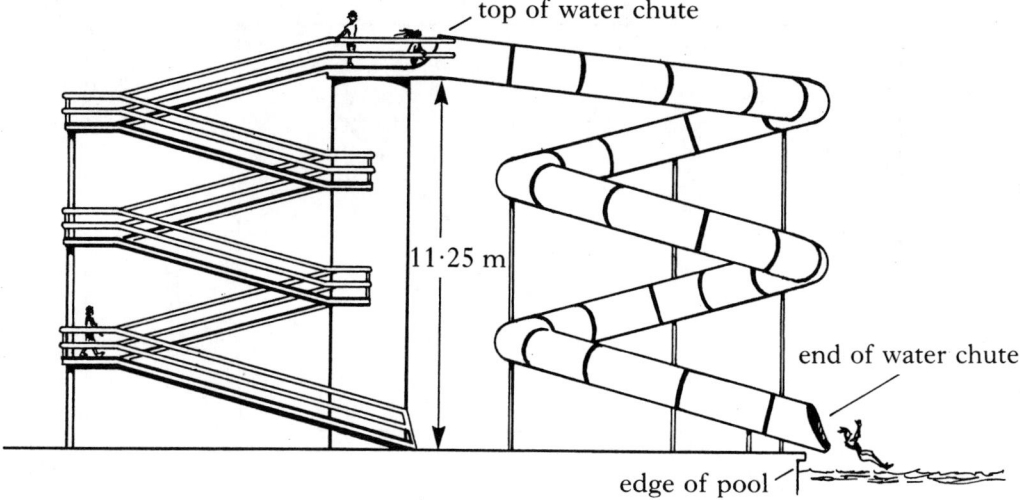

(a) Calculate the potential energy gained by the girl in climbing from the edge of the pool to the top of the chute.

Space for working and answer

(b) The girl slides from rest to the bottom of the chute. Assuming that her potential energy is all transferred to kinetic energy, show that her speed at the bottom of the chute is 15 m/s.

Space for working and answer

(c) Frictional forces act on the girl so that her actual speed at the bottom of the chute is 12 m/s. The graph below shows how the girl's speed varies with time as she slides down the chute.

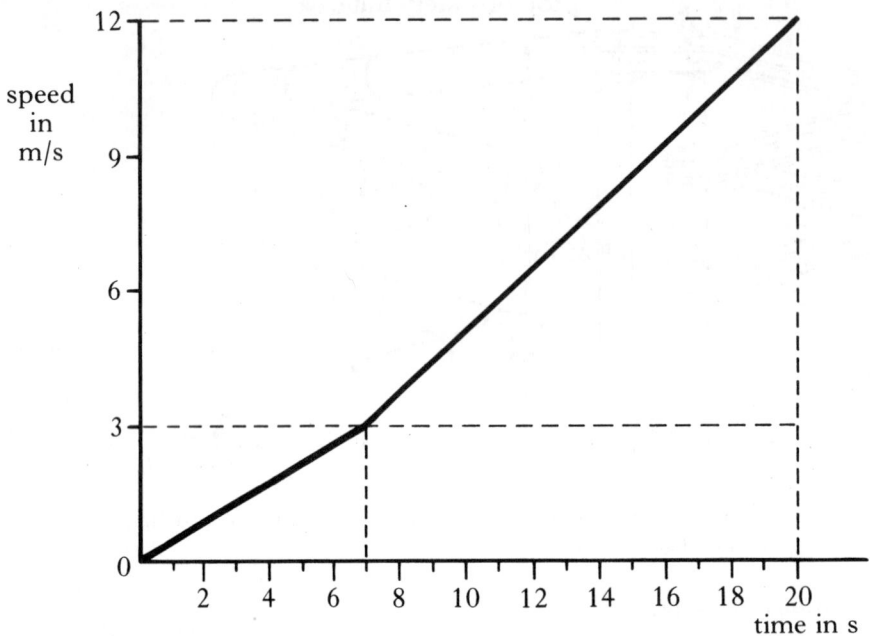

(i) Calculate the distance travelled by the girl in sliding from the top to the bottom of the chute.

Space for working and answer

(ii) The energy transferred as heat in her journey down the chute is 2025 J. Calculate the average frictional force acting on the girl.

Space for working and answer

10. A shop window display area is illuminated using a low voltage lighting circuit. The circuit consists of a transformer and six lamps each rated at 12 V, 50 W connected as shown below.

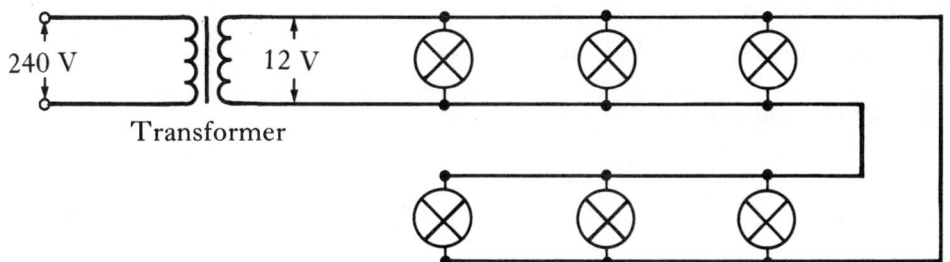

The transformer converts the 240 V mains voltage to the 12 V required to operate the lamps.

(a) Assume that the lamps are operating at their correct rating and the transformer is 100% efficient.

   (i) Calculate the current in **one** of the lamps.

   Space for working and answer

   (ii) Calculate the current drawn from the transformer.

   Space for working and answer

   (iii) Calculate the current drawn from the mains supply.

   Space for working and answer

(b) Give **one** reason why transformers are not 100% efficient.

11. (*a*) A space shuttle of mass 2.1×10^6 kg lifts off from Earth. At lift-off, the force on the shuttle due to air resistance is zero.

(i) Calculate the weight of the shuttle at lift-off.

Space for working and answer

(ii) On the diagram below, label the forces acting on the shuttle at lift-off and show their direction.

(iii) Explain why the speed of a spacecraft, travelling in outer space, is constant although its engines are switched off.

....

....

(*b*) A space shuttle is used to launch a satellite.

(i) The period of the satellite's orbit is 12 hours.

State what would have to happen to the height of the orbit to make it geostationary.

....

(b) (ii) The satellite has solar panels, as shown below, which use solar power to produce electricity.

solar panels

The solar power received on each square metre of panel is 1·5 kW.

The total area of the panels is 12 m² and their efficiency is 10%.

Calculate the electrical power from the panels.

Space for working and answer

(c) During re-entry to the Earth's atmosphere, the temperature of the heat shield of the shuttle rises by 1300 °C. The heat shield has a mass of 3500 kg and gains $4·7 \times 10^9$ J of heat.

(i) Calculate the specific heat capacity of the heat shield.

Space for working and answer

(ii) Using the Data sheet, identify the material of which the shield is made.

....

12. (a) The diagram shows a refracting telescope.

(i) The eyepiece lens can be used as a magnifying glass.

Complete the diagram below to show how a magnified image of an object is formed. The points marked F are one focal length from the centre of the lens.

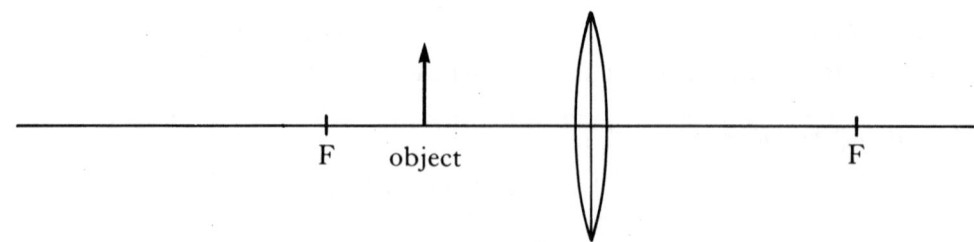

(ii) How could the design of the telescope be altered to increase the brightness of the image when viewing a star?

....

(b) The Hubble telescope was put in orbit around the Earth in 1990.

(i) The telescope uses a curved mirror to collect light rays from a star as shown below.

Complete the diagram to show what happens to the rays of light after they reach the mirror.

(b) (ii) The telescope has detectors for various radiations.

Name a possible detector for ultraviolet radiation.

....

(iii) The spectral lines of radiation from a distant star are shown in figure 1. Figure 2 shows the spectral lines of a number of elements.

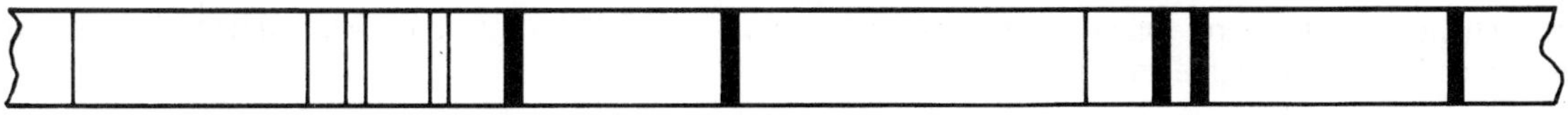

figure 1

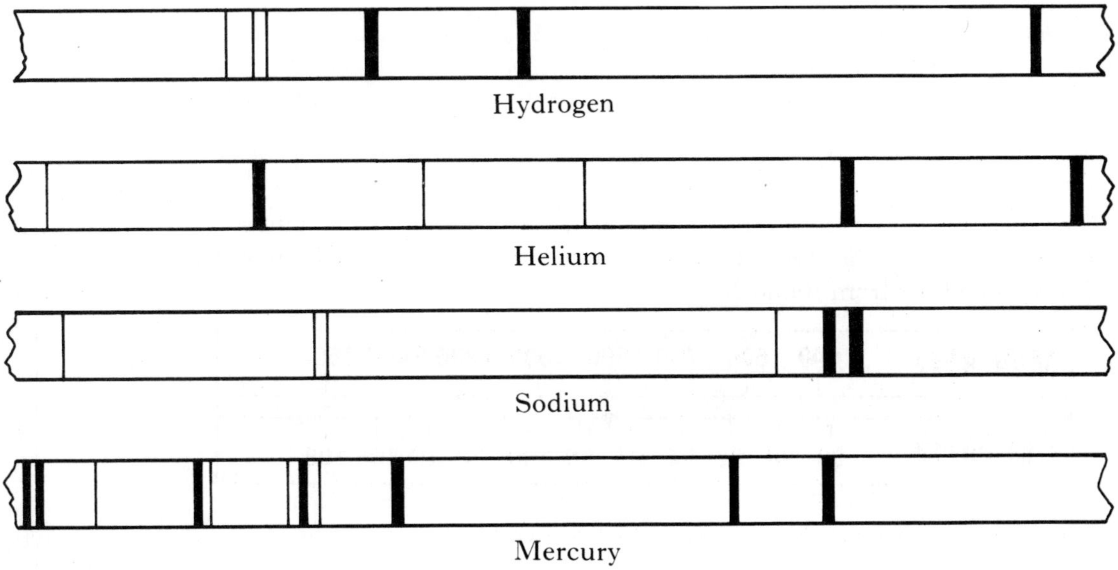

Hydrogen

Helium

Sodium

Mercury

figure 2

Use the spectral lines of the elements in figure 2 to identify which elements are present in the star.

....

[END OF QUESTION PAPER]

SCOTTISH CERTIFICATE OF EDUCATION
1995

WEDNESDAY, 17 MAY
1.30 PM – 3.15 PM

PHYSICS
STANDARD GRADE
Credit Level

1. All questions should be answered.

2. The questions may be answered in any order but all answers must be written clearly and legibly in this book.

3. Write your answer where indicated by the question or in the space provided after the question.

4. If you change your mind about your answer you may score it out and rewrite it in the space provided at the end of the answer book.

5. Before leaving the examination room you must give this book to the Invigilator. If you do not, you may lose all the marks for this paper.

6. Any necessary data will be found in the **data sheet**.

---

1. (*a*) The diagram below shows the display panel on a radio. The pointer on the display is set so that the radio is tuned to receive a medium wave (MW) broadcast from Radio X.

| MW kHz | 540 600 700 800 1000 1200 1400 1600 |
| FM MHz | 88 90 92 94 96 98 100 102 104 106 108 |

(i) On which frequency does Radio X broadcast?

.... (1)

(ii) Calculate the wavelength of the broadcast from Radio X.

Space for working and answer

(2)

(b) An engineer is checking the operation of the transmitter of Radio X. A test audio signal is produced for transmission. The modulated electrical signal in the transmitter is displayed on an oscilloscope as shown in the diagram opposite.

Without adjusting the controls, the engineer uses the oscilloscope to display the traces of the three signals described in parts (i), (ii) and (iii) below.

In the spaces provided, draw the trace which would be observed for each signal.

(i) The audio signal only is displayed.

(1)

(ii) The unmodulated signal used to produce the radio carrier wave is now displayed.

(1)

(iii) Radio X can also broadcast on the Long Wave (LW) band. The same test audio signal is produced for transmission on LW.

The trace of this modulated signal is displayed.

(2)

(c) A person in a cottage, surrounded by hills, wishes to tune in to Radio X. Which of the wavebands, LW or MW, is likely to provide the better reception? Explain your answer.

....

....

....

.... **(2)**

2. The diagram below shows one of the lighting circuits and one of the power ring circuits in a home. The earth wire is not shown in the diagram.

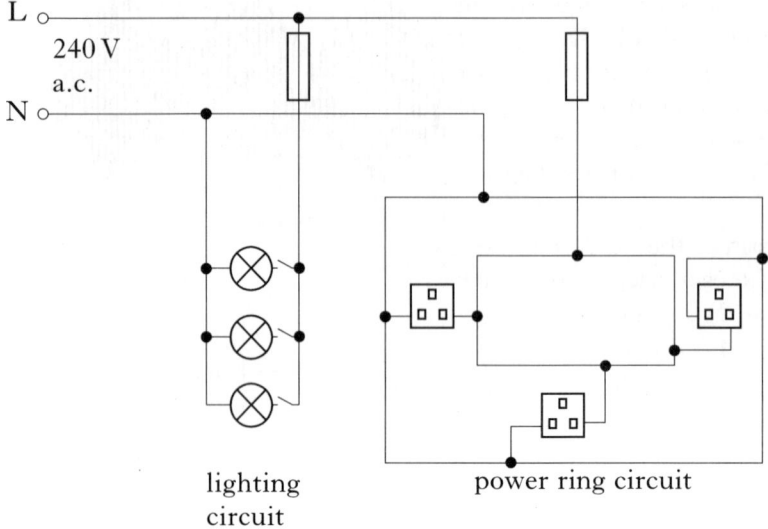

lighting circuit   power ring circuit

(a) In the lighting circuit, the lamps are connected in parallel.

   (i) Give **one** advantage of connecting the lamps in parallel rather than in series.

   ....

   .... (1)

   (ii) One lamp has a resistance of 900 Ω and each of the other two has a resistance of 600 Ω.

   Calculate the resistance of the lighting circuit when all the lamps are switched on.

   Space for working and answer

   (2)

(b) State **one** advantage of connecting the power sockets in a ring circuit.

   ....

   .... (1)

(c) The mains fuses protect the wiring in each circuit. A circuit breaker can be used instead of a fuse.

Give **one** reason why a circuit breaker may be preferred to a fuse.

....

.... (1)

3. (a) A diagram of a rating plate on a hair drier is shown below.

> Electronic   Model No. 272
>
> 240 V ∿ 50 Hz
>
> 1200 W

(i) A suitable flex has to be connected to the hair drier.

(A) Which **one** of the following flexes, P, Q, R and S, is the most appropriate for connection to the hair drier?

P — 3 A rating
Q — 3 A rating
R — 13 A rating
S — 13 A rating

Answer [   ] (1)

(B) Give **two** reasons for your choice in part (A).

Reason 1: ....

....

Reason 2: ....

.... (2)

(ii) Calculate the resistance of the hair drier when operating at its stated rating.

Space for working and answer

(3)

(iii) The hair drier has a fan which is driven by an electric motor. Parts of this motor are shown in the diagram below.

On the diagram, label the field coils. **(1)**

(b) A diagram of a simple d.c. electric motor is shown below.

(i) State what is used instead of field coils in this motor.

.... **(1)**

(ii) When there is a current in the coil, a downward force acts on part AB and an upward force on part CD.
What causes these forces to be in opposite directions?

....

.... **(1)**

(iii) Describe how the commutator and the brushes allow the coil to keep spinning.

....

....

....

.... **(2)**

4. A patient is examined to find out if his kidneys are working properly. A liquid containing some gamma emitting radioactive material is injected into the patient's bloodstream. This radioactive material and other impurities should be absorbed by the kidney and then passed to the patient's bladder. A gamma camera is used to detect the radiation coming from the patient's kidneys. The gamma camera produces images of the patient's left and right kidneys on a monitor as shown below.

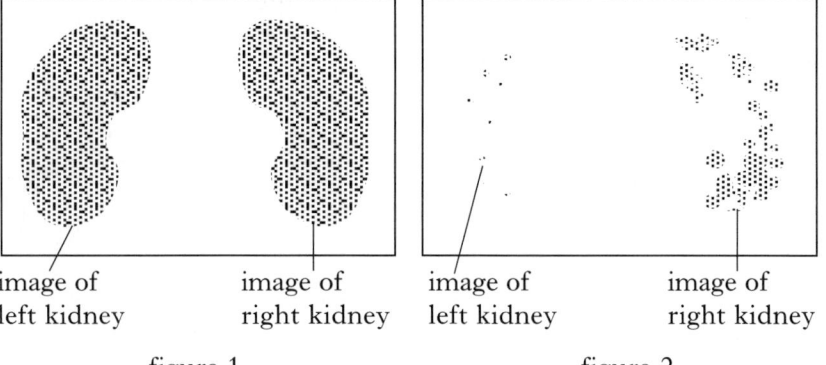

figure 1   figure 2

Figure 1 shows the image produced 2 minutes after the injection and figure 2 shows the image 10 minutes after the injection.

(a) Which kidney is not working properly? Explain your answer.

....

....

....

.... (2)

(b) The half-lives of four gamma emitters W, X, Y and Z are listed in the table below.

Gamma emitter	Half life
W	1 minute
X	5 minutes
Y	5 hours
Z	5 days

The examination of the patient lasts for 15 minutes.

Which one of the above gamma emitters would be most suitable for use in the examination?

.... (1)

(c) Alpha emitting materials are never injected into the body in order to obtain images of parts of the body.

State **two** reasons why alpha emitting materials are unsuitable.

Reason 1: ....

....

Reason 2: ....

.... **(2)**

5. (a) X-ray machines, as shown in figure 1, are used to destroy cancerous tissue in the body of a patient. The X-rays produced by the machine reach the patient from different directions by rotating the machine around the patient's body.

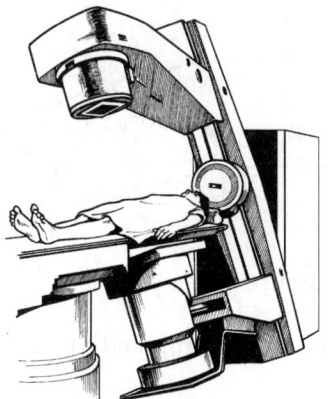

figure 1

In this treatment, the X-rays are not fired continuously in one direction. The different paths of the X-rays through the patient's body are shown in figure 2.

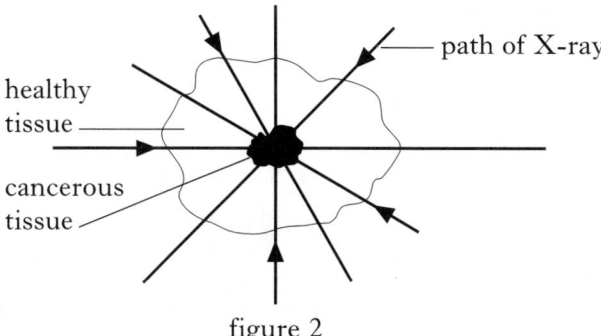

figure 2

(i) Explain why rotating the X-ray machine provides a safer way of ensuring that the cancerous tissue receives the maximum dose.

....

....

....

.... (2)

(ii) Why is it important that the patient keeps still during the treatment?

....

.... (1)

(b) After using the X-ray machine, an optical fibre is used to view the tissue inside the patient's body. Figure 3 shows the path of a ray of light as it passes along part of the optical fibre.

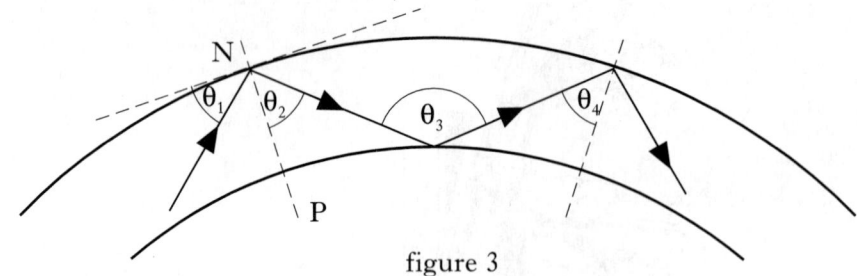

figure 3

(i) Which of the angles, θ_1, θ_2, θ_3, and θ_4, marked on the diagram, is an angle of incidence?

.... **(1)**

(ii) What name is given to the dotted line NP?

.... **(1)**

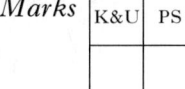

6. A student connects the following circuit in order to find the power gain of an amplifier.

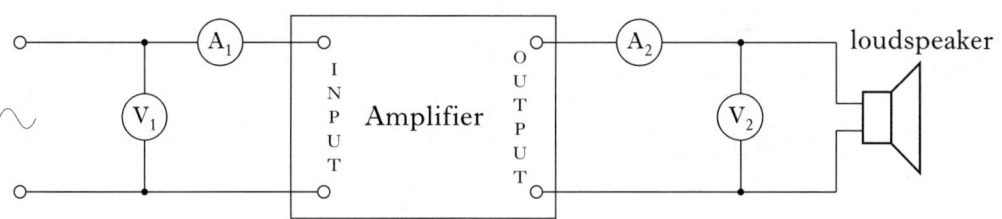

The readings on the meters shown in the circuit diagram are given below.

| Reading on V_1 = 0·2 V | Reading on V_2 = 2·0 V |
| Reading on A_1 = 0·005 A | Reading on A_2 = 0·04 A |

(a) Calculate the power gain of the amplifier.

Space for working and answer

(3)

(b) The frequency of the input signal is 100 Hz.
What is the frequency of the output signal?

.... (1)

7. A pupil builds the following light detecting circuit to sense the level of brightness in a room.

V_1 is the input voltage to the transistor. The transistor switches fully on when V_1 rises above 0·7 V.

(a) Initially the level of brightness in the room is very low. At this brightness the resistance of the LDR is 1800 Ω and the LED is off.

   (i) Calculate the value of the input voltage V_1.

   Space for working and answer (2)

   (ii) What is the value of the voltage V_2 across the LDR?

   Space for working and answer (1)

(b) The pupil increases the brightness in the room.

   (i) What happens to the resistance of the LDR? (1)

   (ii) State what happens to the values of V_2 and V_1. (2)

   (iii) Explain why the LED lights up. (2)

8. The Smith family want to install a porch lamp which will automatically switch on at night but only if a master switch is closed. The Smiths think that they can design a circuit which uses logic gates to solve the problem. Their first attempt at a design is shown in the diagram below.

When the light sensor goes from being in dark to being in light, the logic level at X changes from logic 0 to logic 1.

When the master switch is turned from off to on, the logic level at Y changes from logic 0 to logic 1.

(a) Name the logic gate G used by the Smiths in their design.

.... **(1)**

(b) Complete the truth table below to show the logic levels at Z in the above diagram.

X	Y	Z
0	0	
0	1	
1	0	
1	1	

(2)

(c) Give **one** reason why the Smiths' design is **not** suitable.

....

.... **(1)**

(d) What alteration could you make to the design so that it will operate as required?

.... **(1)**

9. A keen walker bought a device called a pedometer to find out how far he walks during his journeys. The instructions ask him to measure the length of his step and enter this information into the pedometer. The pedometer detects and counts the number of steps taken and then uses the information which has been entered to calculate and display the distance walked.

(a) After walking for 30 minutes, the pedometer displays a distance of 2520 m.

Calculate the walker's average speed, in **kilometres per hour**, during this time.

Space for working and answer

(2)

(b) In order to provide the information on the length of step which had to be entered into the pedometer, the walker measured his step from the back of his heel to the front of his toes as shown below.

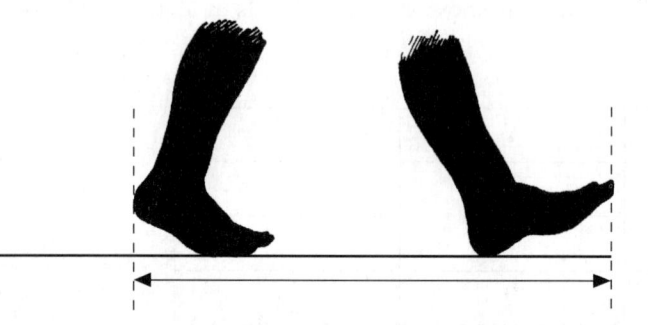

During his journey, the walker did not change the length of his step. The actual distance walked was not 2520 m as displayed on the pedometer.

State whether the actual distance walked was greater or smaller than 2520 m. Explain your answer.

....

....

....

.... (2)

(c) What changes would you make to the measurement so that the information entered into the pedometer would allow it to record the actual distance walked?

....

.... (1)

10. Competitors are taking part in a bobsleigh competition.

(a) Figure 1 shows the bobsleigh at point X near the end of its run.

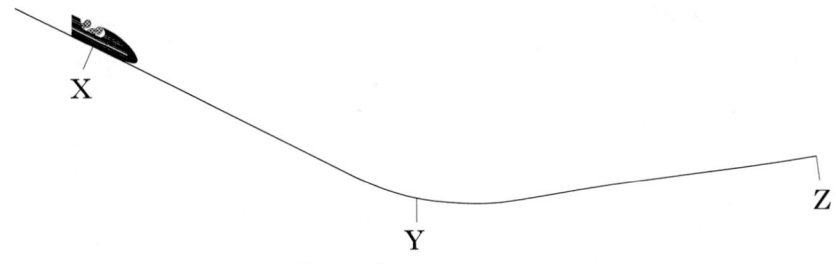

figure 1

When the bobsleigh reaches point Y, the brakes are applied until it comes to rest at point Z.

The speed–time graph of the motion of the bobsleigh from point X to point Z is shown in figure 2.

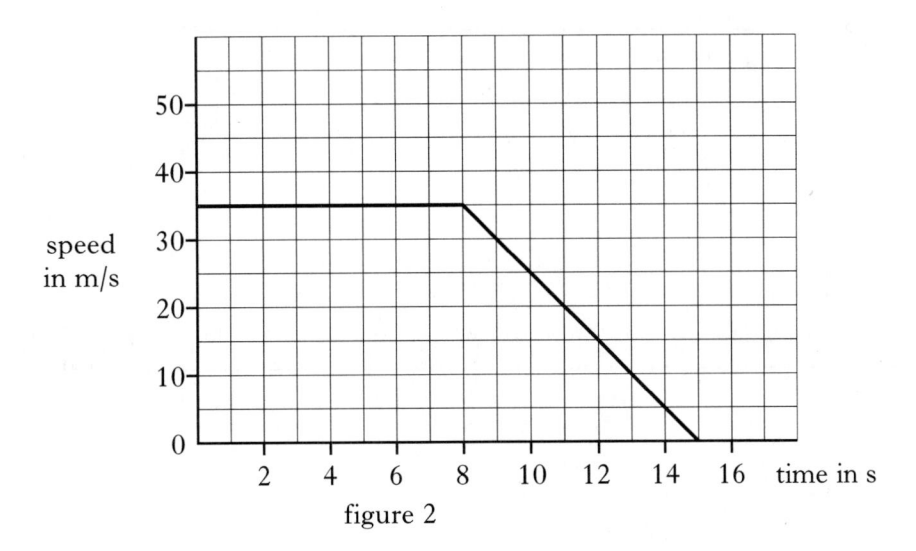

figure 2

(i) What time did the bobsleigh take to travel from X to Y?

.... (1)

(ii) What was the distance travelled by the bobsleigh from point X until it came to rest?

Space for working and answer

(3)

(iii) Calculate the deceleration of the bobsleigh between Y and Z.

Space for working and answer

(2)

(iv) The competitors and the bobsleigh have a total mass of 380 kg.
Calculate the force causing the deceleration of the competitors and bobsleigh.

Space for working and answer

(2)

(b) At the start of a run, at point A in figure 3, both competitors push the empty bobsleigh. At point B, one of the competitors jumps in while the other keeps pushing. At point C, the second competitor jumps in.

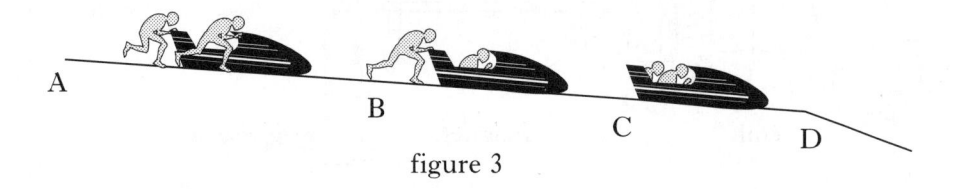

figure 3

The speed–time graph of the motion of the bobsleigh from A to C is shown in figure 4.

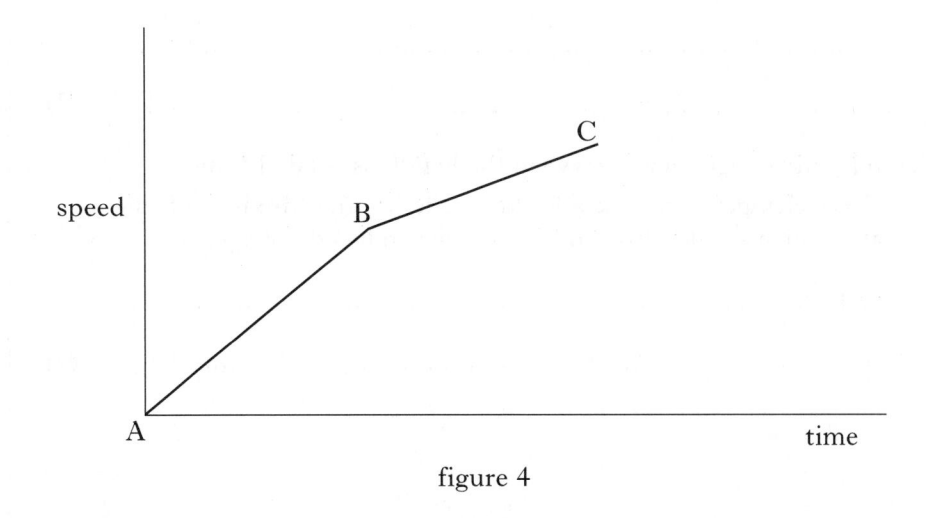

figure 4

(i) Give **two** reasons, in terms of Newton's laws, for the change in the acceleration of the bobsleigh between AB and BC.

Reason 1: ....

....

Reason 2: ....

.... (2)

(ii) Complete the graph in figure 4 to show how the speed varies with time between **C** and **D** when both competitors are in the bobsleigh. (1)

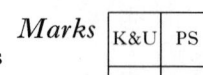

11. (a) The diagram below shows a simple hand operated generator which is used to light a lamp.

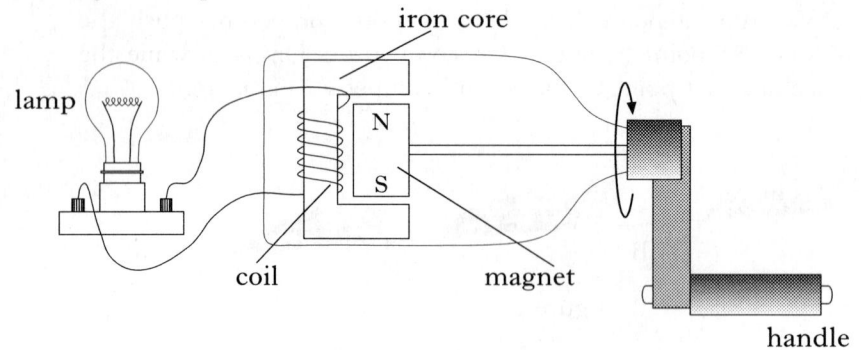

(i) Explain why a voltage is induced across the coil of the generator when the handle is turned.

....

.... **(1)**

(ii) The induced voltage increases when the handle is rotated faster.

State **two** changes which could be made to the **design** of the generator which would also produce a larger induced voltage.

Change 1: ....

Change 2: .... **(2)**

(b) A power station generates electricity by using large a.c. generators. Electricity from the power station is transmitted across country using the National Grid system. Parts of this system are shown in the diagram below.

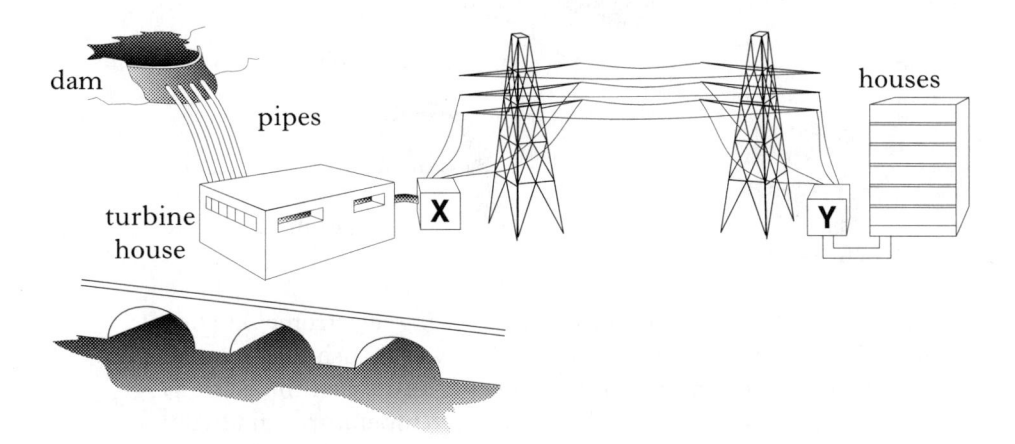

(i) Name the parts labelled **X** and **Y** and describe the purpose of each.

Part **X**: ....

....

Part **Y**: ....

.... (2)

(ii) A power line in the system has a resistance of 2 Ω for every kilometre length. The power line is 100 km long and carries a current of 200 A.

Calculate the electrical power loss in the line.

Space for working and answer

(3)

12. Marion decides to show her father that she can measure the power of their automatic kettle. She makes use of the equipment shown below.

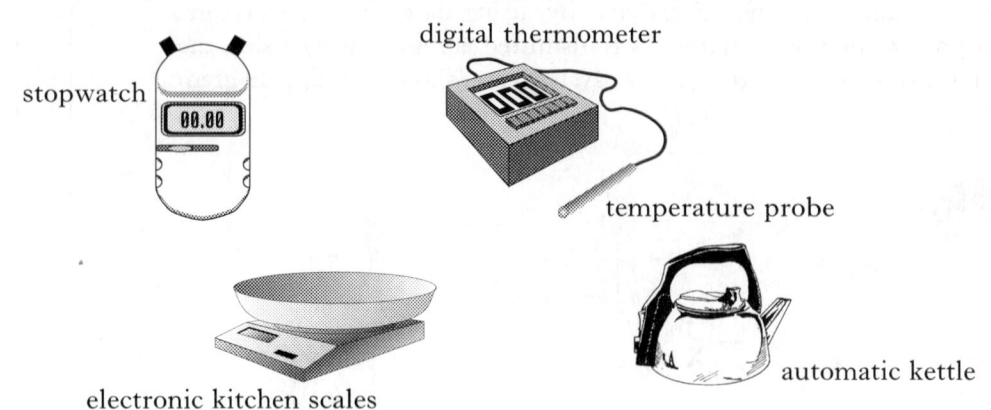

stopwatch

digital thermometer

temperature probe

electronic kitchen scales

automatic kettle

She measures accurately the mass of some water using electronic kitchen scales and reads the initial temperature of the water using a digital thermometer. All of the water is poured into the kettle and when the kettle is switched on she starts a stopwatch. The water temperature gradually increases and eventually, after the water has been boiling for a short time, the kettle switches off automatically. Marion stops the stopwatch at this point.

Marion's measurements are listed below.

Mass of water = 1·52 kg

Initial temperature of water = 19·5 °C

Time for which kettle was switched on = 325 s

(a) Calculate the amount of heat supplied to raise the water temperature to 100 °C.

Space for working and answer

(3)

(b) Use the answer to part (a) to estimate the power of the kettle.
(Use an appropriate number of figures in your answer.)

Space for working and answer

(2)

(c) The rating plate on the kettle indicates that the power rating is 2 kW. Errors in Marion's experimental method cause the calculated value of the power to be different from that shown on the rating plate. One of these errors is due to heat being lost from the water.

(i) Describe **one** other source of error in Marion's method.

....

.... **(1)**

(ii) How could you improve her method so that this other error is reduced?

....

....

....

.... **(1)**

(d) Later, the kettle is switched on again but by mistake the lid is left off. The water reaches boiling point but the autoswitch does not switch off.

If there were no heat losses, how much heat energy would be required to vaporise 0·1 kg of water?

(Specific latent heat of vaporisation of water = $22·6 \times 10^5$ J/kg)

Space for working and answer

(2)

13. (*a*) A telescope may be used to look at distant objects such as stars. A simple refracting telescope is shown below.

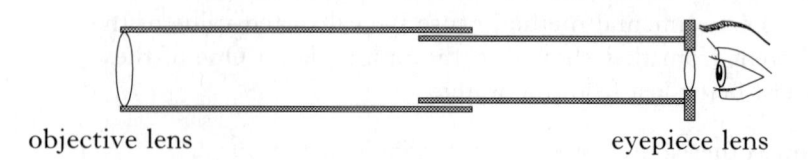

objective lens   eyepiece lens

(i) A pupil replaces the objective lens in the telescope by one of identical focal length but having a smaller diameter as shown below.

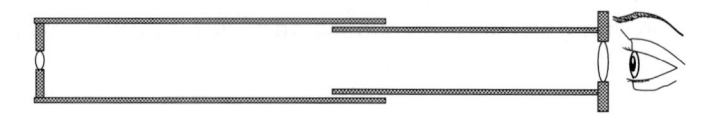

Explain the effect this has on the image of the object seen through the telescope.

....

....

.... **(2)**

(ii) The pupil removes the objective lens from the telescope and uses it to produce an image of an object on a screen.

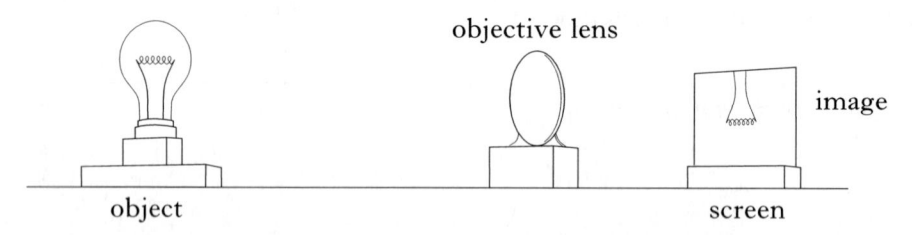

object   objective lens   screen   image

Complete the diagram below to show how the lens forms an image of the object. Clearly show the position of this image on your diagram.

The points marked F are one focal length from the centre of the lens.

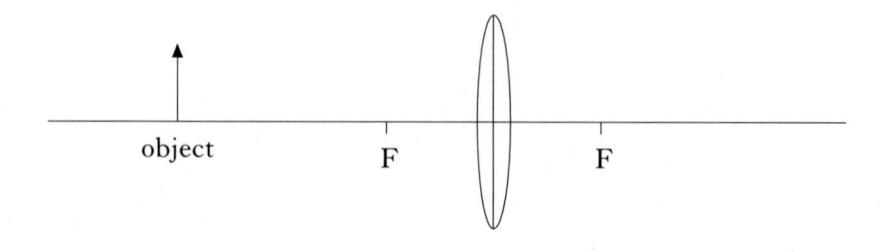

object   F   F

(3)

(b) The radiation emitted by a star forms part of the electromagnetic spectrum. Part of the electromagnetic spectrum is shown below. Two radiations, P and Q, have not been named.

Gamma	X–ray	P	Visible	Q	Microwave	Radio–TV

Frequency (Hz): 10^{21}, 10^{17}, 10^{16}, 10^{14}, 10^{12}, 10^{10}, 10^{6}

(i) Name each of the radiations P and Q.

Radiation P: ....

Radiation Q: .... **(1)**

(ii) One type of radiation in the electromagnetic spectrum has a wavelength of 300 m.

Using information from the data sheet and the electromagnetic spectrum above, determine the name of this radiation.

You **must** show clearly the calculation you used to arrive at your conclusion.

Space for working and answer

(3)

(c) Radio waves emitted by stars can be detected on Earth using a radio telescope similar to that shown below.

Describe how the curved reflector and the position of the detector on the radio telescope ensure that a strong signal is picked up.

....

....

....

.... (2)

14. (a) A meteor is a rock which travels through space.

One particular meteor is travelling through space at a speed of 70 000 m/s. The mass of the meteor is 2 kg.

Calculate its kinetic energy.

Space for working and answer

(2)

(b) While the meteor travels through space, it is not normally seen from Earth by the naked eye. If, by chance, the meteor enters the Earth's atmosphere, it may be seen as a bright streak of light in the night sky.

Explain why the meteor appears as a streak of light.

....

.... (2)

[END OF QUESTION PAPER]

SCOTTISH CERTIFICATE OF EDUCATION 1996

FRIDAY, 17 MAY 1.30 PM – 3.15 PM

PHYSICS
STANDARD GRADE
Credit Level

Marks

1. Later this year, the Olympic Games will be held in the city of Atlanta in the United States of America (USA).

   (a) Television pictures of the Games will be transmitted from the USA to Britain. The TV signals will be carried by microwaves. The microwaves will travel from the USA to Britain via a geostationary satellite positioned 36 000 km above the surface of the Earth as shown in the diagram below.

   (i) What is meant by saying that the satellite is geostationary?

   ....

   .... (2)

   (ii) The frequency of the microwaves to be used in the transmission is 12 GHz.

   Calculate the wavelength of the microwaves used in the transmission.

   Space for working and answer

   (2)

(b) Newspaper reporters at the games will be able to fax their reports back to Britain by a telephone link. The telephone link uses an 8000 km length of glass optical fibre. The telephone signals are carried by light which is transmitted through the glass fibre.

How long will it take the telephone signals to travel from the USA to Britain?

Space for working and answer

(3)

2. A remote control device for a television set has buttons which are used to produce signals to change the channels, the brightness and the colour of the picture. The remote control has an infrared transmitter as shown in the diagram below.

The signals are carried by the infrared radiation from the transmitter to a detector on the TV set.

(a) Name a detector of infrared radiation.

.... **(1)**

(b) The channel buttons on the remote control are used to change to different stations on the TV.

Which part of the TV circuit selects one particular station?

.... **(1)**

(c) Describe what happens inside the tube of the TV set when the brightness control button is pressed to increase the brightness of the picture on the screen.

....

....

....

.... **(2)**

(d) The screen of a colour TV is made up of red, green and blue phosphor dots which glow to produce colours on the screen.

Which phosphor dots will glow if the screen is

(i) white; ....

(ii) yellow? .... **(2)**

(e) Describe how different shades of yellow are produced on the screen.

....

....

.... **(2)**

3. The diagram below shows a simplified version of part of the lighting system of a car. The negative terminal of the battery is connected to the metal body of the car at X.

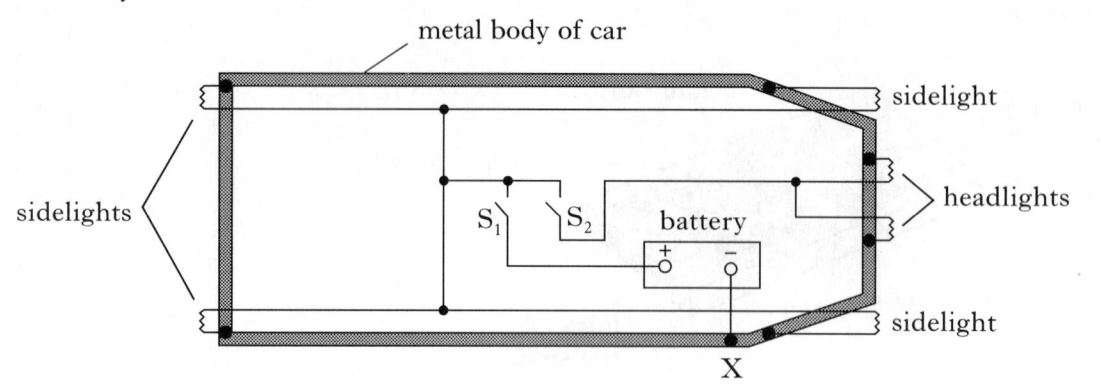

(a) Which lights, if any, are on when:

(i) switch S_1 alone is closed; ....

(ii) switch S_2 alone is closed? .... **(1)**

(b) The sidelights are rated at 12V, 5W and the headlights at 12V, 21W.

(i) Calculate the current drawn from the battery when all the sidelights and headlights are switched on.

Space for working and answer

(3)

(ii) Explain which type of light, sidelight or headlight, has the lower resistance.

....

....

.... **(2)**

(c) The diagram below shows how the brakelights of the car are connected to the battery. S_3 is the ignition switch of the car and S_4 is the switch which is closed when the brake pedal is pressed.

The owner of the car wishes to install a third brakelight Z in the back window of the car. Connection points to the electric circuit are available at A, B, C and D as shown.

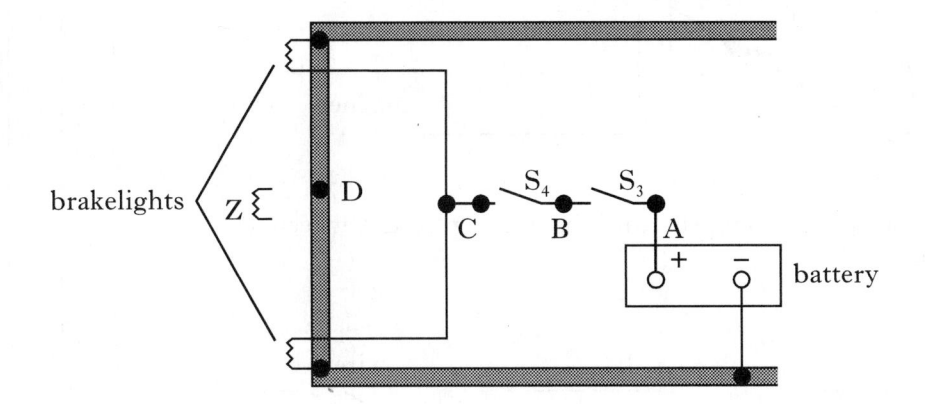

Complete the diagram above to show the points to which the brakelight Z should be connected so that it comes on only when the brake pedal is pressed and the ignition switch is closed.

(1)

4. (*a*) A current carrying wire is placed between the poles of a magnet. The direction of the electron current in the wire is as indicated in figure 1. The conductor experiences an upward force as shown in figure 1.

figure 1

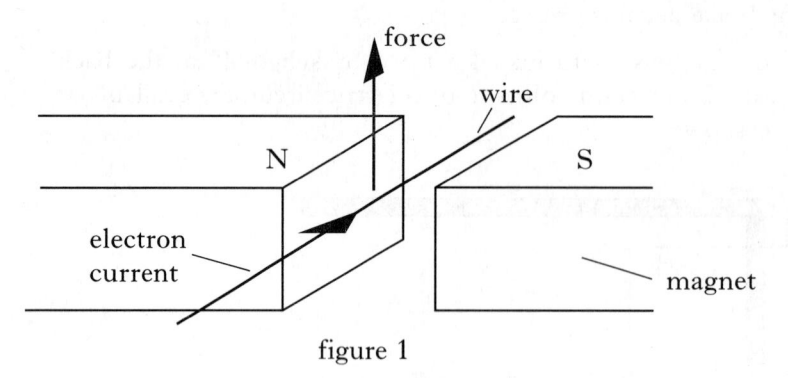

Figures 2 and 3 show other current carrying wires placed between the poles of magnets.

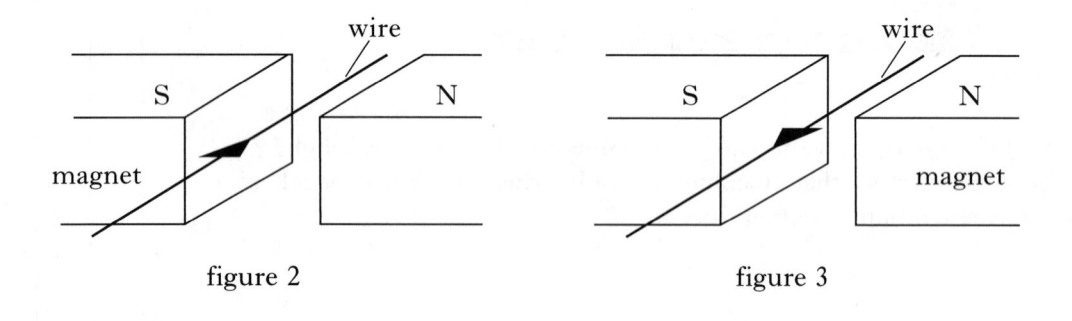

figure 2   figure 3

In each case, indicate on figures 2 and 3 the direction of the force on the wire.

(2)

(b) Figure 4 shows a simple electric motor with a coil WXYZ free to spin about a shaft PQ.

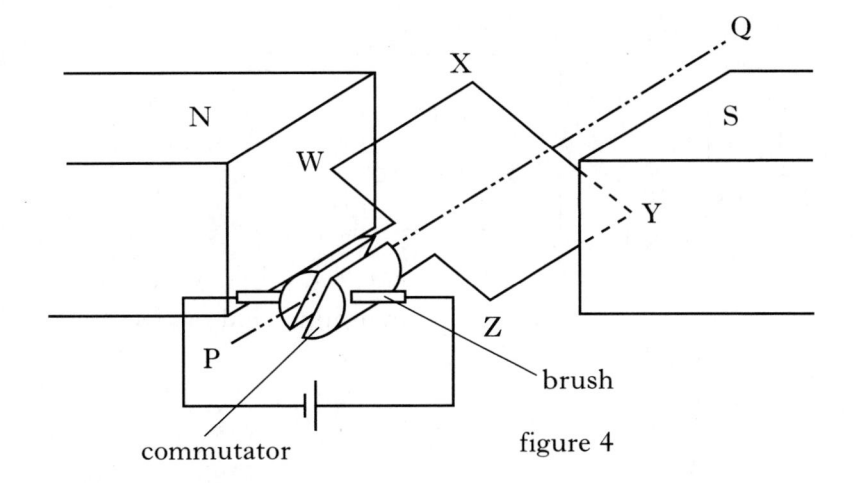

figure 4

(i) By looking at the diagram and using the conclusions you reached in part (a), mark on figure 4 above:

  (A) the direction of the electron current in the coil;

  (B) the directions of the forces on the coil;

  (C) the direction of rotation of the coil. (3)

(ii) Describe how the brushes and the commutator allow the coil to keep spinning.

....

....

....

....

.... (3)

(c) In commercial motors, explain why:

  (i) more than one rotating coil is used;

  .... (1)

  (ii) field coils rather than permanent magnets are used.

  .... (1)

5. During a game, a player injures a knee. An X-ray is taken to check whether the leg has been broken. Ultrasound is used to determine if any fluid has formed in the knee. Figure 1 shows the position of the X-ray transmitter and figure 2 the position of the ultrasound transmitter and receiver in front of the knee.

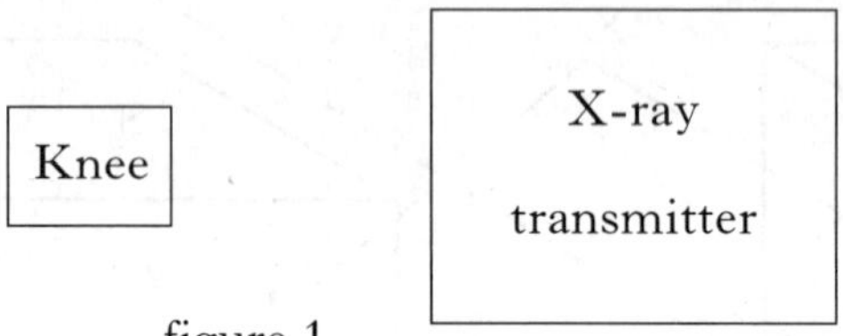

figure 1

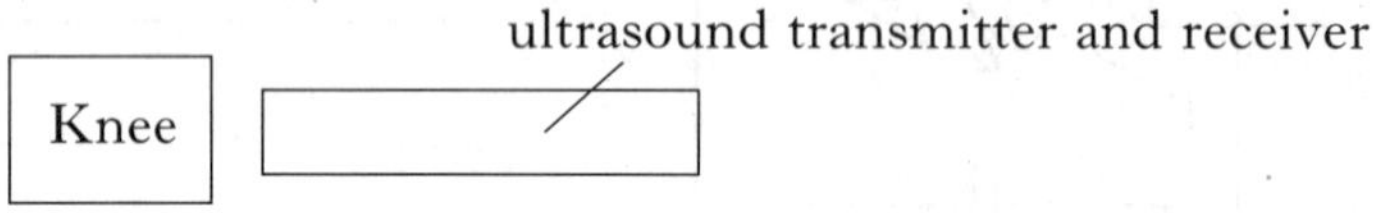

figure 2

(a) (i) Indicate on figure 1 where the receiver for the X-rays should be placed. **(1)**

(ii) State why the ultrasound transmitter and receiver are on the same side of the knee as shown in figure 2.

....

.... **(1)**

(iii) It is decided to treat the knee injury using ultrasound to speed the healing process. The ultrasound used in the treatment has a power of 8 W. The energy to be delivered to the site of the injury is 2400 J at each treatment.

How many minutes should each treatment last?

Space for working and answer

(2)

(b) Read the following passage.

The limit of human hearing is 20 kHz but other animals, such as bats and dolphins, make use of sound in the 30–100 kHz range. Sound above the range of human hearing is called ultrasound. Ultrasound behaves in a similar manner to audible sound, having a speed of 340 m/s in air, a speed of 1500 m/s in soft tissue and a speed of 4100 m/s in bone. Ultrasound is used not only to diagnose the cause of an injury but also to help in the healing of injuries. When used in the healing process absorption of the ultrasound takes place.

(i) State the lowest frequency of ultrasound.

.... (1)

(ii) What is the speed of ultrasound in soft tissue?

.... (1)

(iii) State whether energy is absorbed or reflected when ultrasound is used to help the healing process.

.... (1)

6. A school Physics department owns a number of radioactive sources.

(a) When carrying out an experiment, a teacher placed a radioactive source in front of a detector.

After allowing for background radiation, the following observations were made.

1. Placing a sheet of paper between the source and the detector greatly reduced the reading on the detector.
2. Placing a block of lead 2 cm thick between the source and the detector reduced the reading on the detector to zero.

A pupil suggested that the source was emitting only alpha and gamma radiation.

Explain whether or not the pupil's suggestion is correct.

....
....
....
.... (2)

(b) Describe briefly a precaution which should be taken when working with radioactive sources.

....
.... (1)

(c) The teacher set up an experiment, as shown in the diagram below, to determine the half life of another radioactive source. Before the source was placed in position, it was noted that there was a reading on the counter.

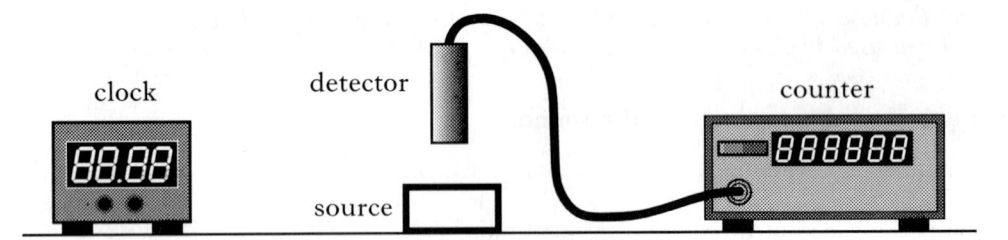

The source was placed in position and the count rate noted at the start of the experiment and again at regular intervals.

A pupil suggested that the half life of the source might be found from the time taken for the count rate to drop to half its original value.

(i) Explain why the pupil's suggestion may not give an accurate value for the half life.

.... (1)

(ii) How could the half life of the source be determined from the experiment described above?

....
....
.... (2)

(d) The source used in the above experiment had an original activity of 800 kBq and a half life of 30 s.

Calculate the activity of the source after 2 minutes.

Space for working and answer

(2)

7. The diagram below shows an automatic hand washing unit in a restaurant.

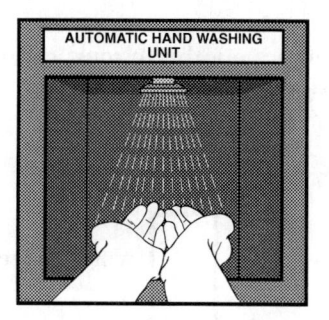

figure 1

Inserting the hands into the unit breaks a light beam and causes a stream of water to be turned on for ten seconds.

(a) The light beam is directed at a light dependent resistor (LDR) which is part of the circuit shown in figure 2.

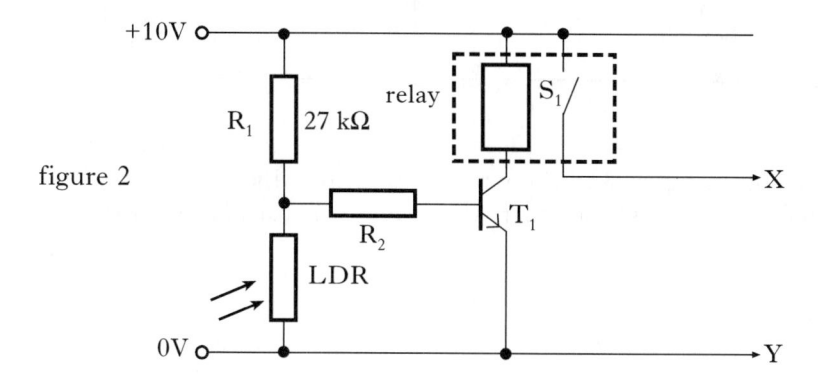

figure 2

(i) When hands are inserted into the unit, the circuit in figure 2 causes the switch S_1 in the relay to close. Explain why this happens.

....
....
....
....
.... (3)

(ii) Calculate the voltage across the LDR when its resistance is $9 \cdot 0 \, k\Omega$.

Space for working and answer

(2)

(b) When the relay switch in figure 2 is closed, another circuit connected to X and Y as shown in figure 3 opens a water valve for ten seconds.

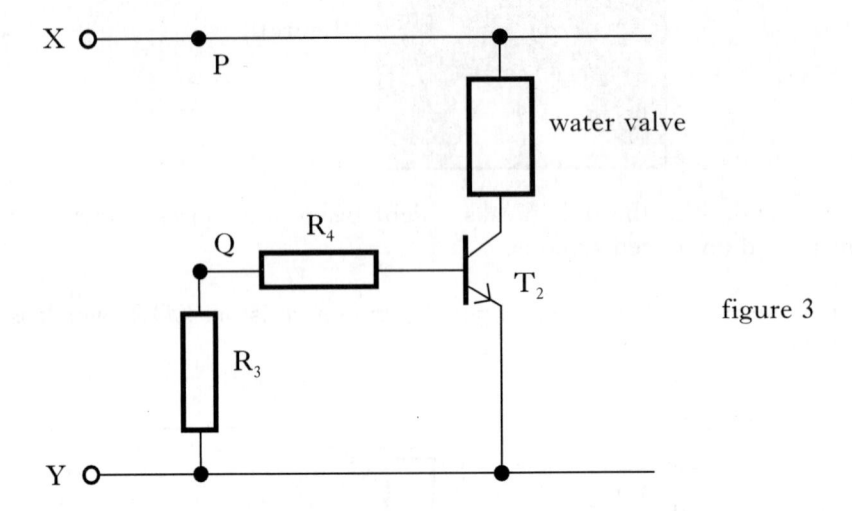

figure 3

Complete the diagram in figure 3 to show the component which should be connected between P and Q so that the water is turned on for ten seconds. **(1)**

8. Traffic engineers use metal loops to detect the number of vehicles travelling along a road. The loops are buried under the road surface. When a vehicle passes over a loop, a single digital pulse is sent to a control circuit. The diagram below shows a situation where traffic must move in single file on each side of a road. Loops X and Y are buried under each side of the road at the positions shown.

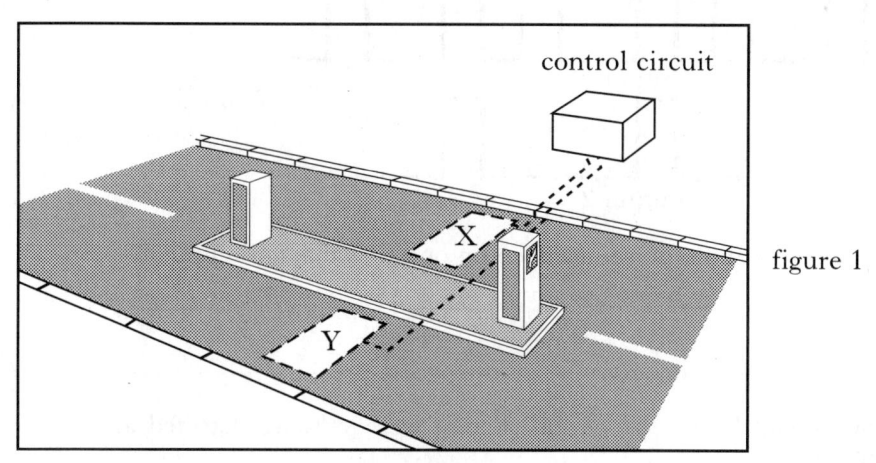

figure 1

(a) Part of the control circuit is shown in figure 2.

During the time a vehicle passes over loop X, the logic level at P changes from logic 0 to logic 1.

During the time a vehicle passes over loop Y, the logic level at Q changes from logic 0 to logic 1.

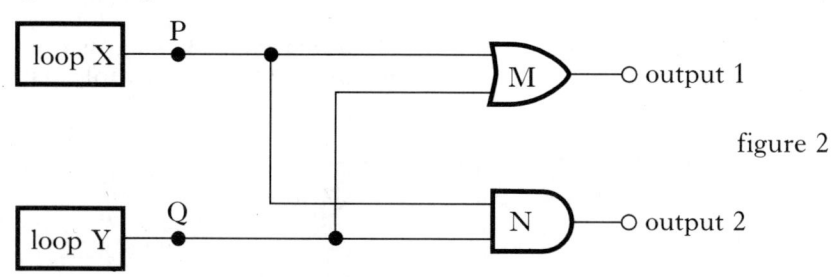

figure 2

(i) Name logic gate M.

.... **(1)**

(ii) Name logic gate N.

.... **(1)**

(iii) Complete the truth table below for this part of the circuit.

Input P	Input Q	Output 1	Output 2
0	0		
0	1		
1	0		
1	1		

(2)

(b) The two outputs from the above circuit are displayed on a computer screen. The outputs observed over a one minute period are shown in figure 3.

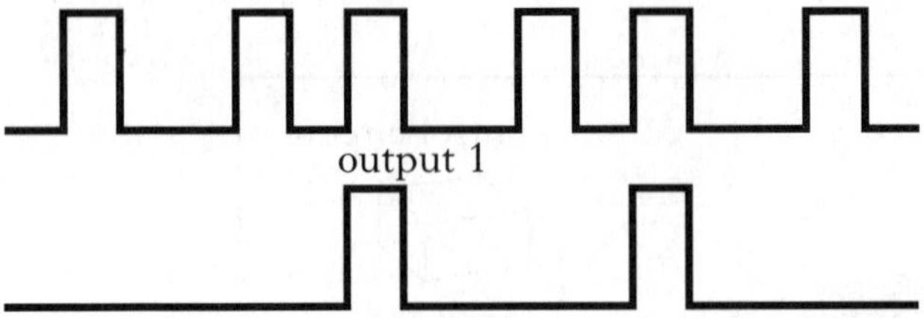

figure 3

(i) Explain why more pulses are seen on output 1 than on output 2.

....

.... (2)

(ii) How often, during the period shown, were vehicles detected at the same time?

.... (1)

(iii) How many vehicles were detected during the period shown?

.... (1)

(c) As shown in figure 4, a light emitting diode (LED) is connected across the 6 V supply of the control circuit, to indicate when the supply is switched on.

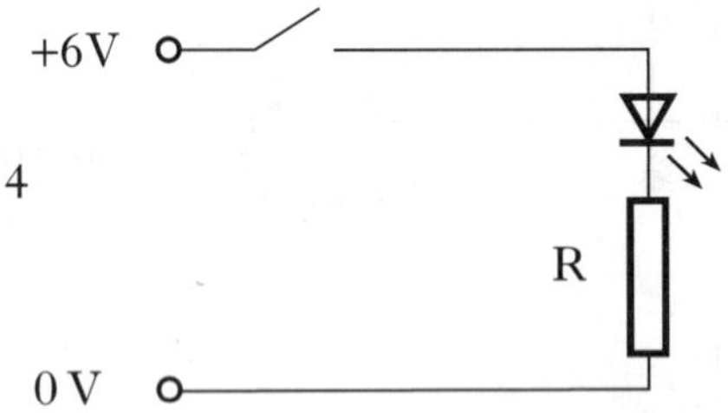

figure 4

When lit, the current in the LED is 20 mA and the voltage across it is 1·6 V.

Calculate the resistance of the resistor R.

Space for working and answer

(3)

9. A competitor takes part in a speed skating race. The competitor takes 50 seconds to complete the race. The graph below shows how the competitor's speed changes with time during the race.

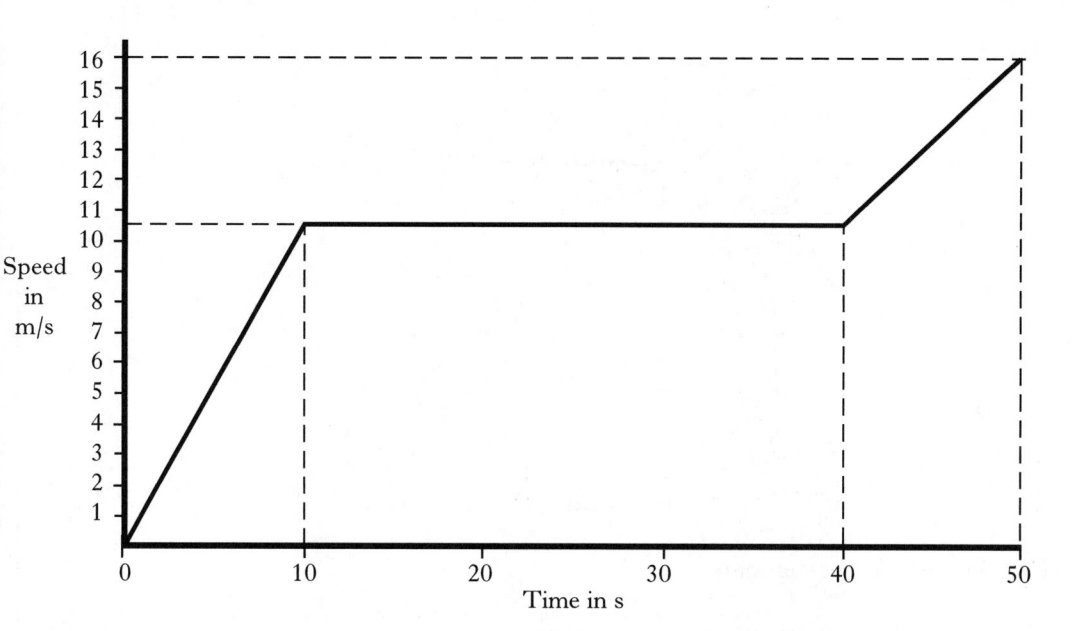

(a) (i) Calculate the acceleration of the skater at the start of the race.

Space for working and answer

(2)

(ii) Calculate the distance over which the skater raced.

Space for working and answer

(3)

(b) The diagram shows the horizontal forces acting on the skater during the race.

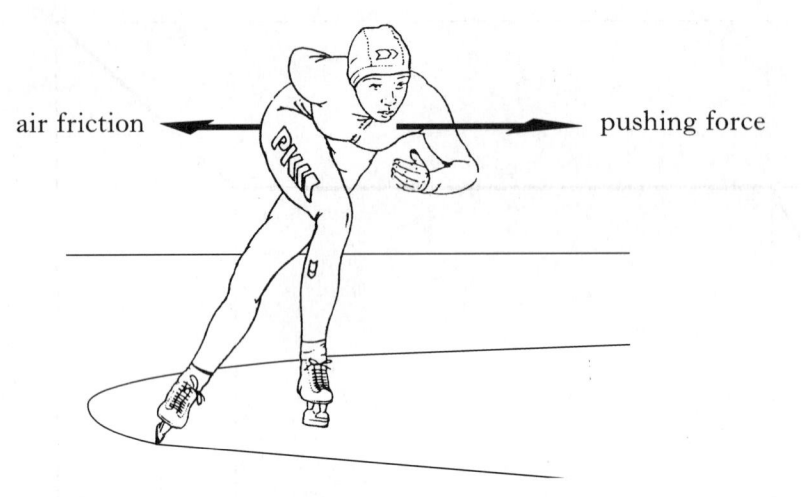

air friction ←　　　　　　　　→ pushing force

(i) How do these forces compare:

(A) during the first 10 seconds of the race;

.... **(1)**

(B) between times of 10 s and 40 s during the race?

.... **(1)**

(ii) Suggest **one** way in which the skater reduces the air friction acting on her during the race.

....

.... **(1)**

10. A child's electric ride-on car is driven up a ramp as shown in the diagram below. The length of the ramp is 20 m and it rises to a height of 2 m above the level surface.

(a) The child and ride-on car have a total mass of 60 kg.

Calculate the potential energy gained by the child and car in travelling from the bottom to the top of the ramp.

Space for working and answer

(2)

(b) The ride-on car takes 25 seconds to travel from the bottom of the ramp to the top.

Ignoring frictional losses, calculate the average power output from the ride-on car motor if the car travels up the ramp at constant speed.

Space for working and answer

(2)

11. A baby's milk bottle is heated using a bottle warmer. The bottle warmer has foam filled walls and a shiny outer casing as shown in the diagram below.

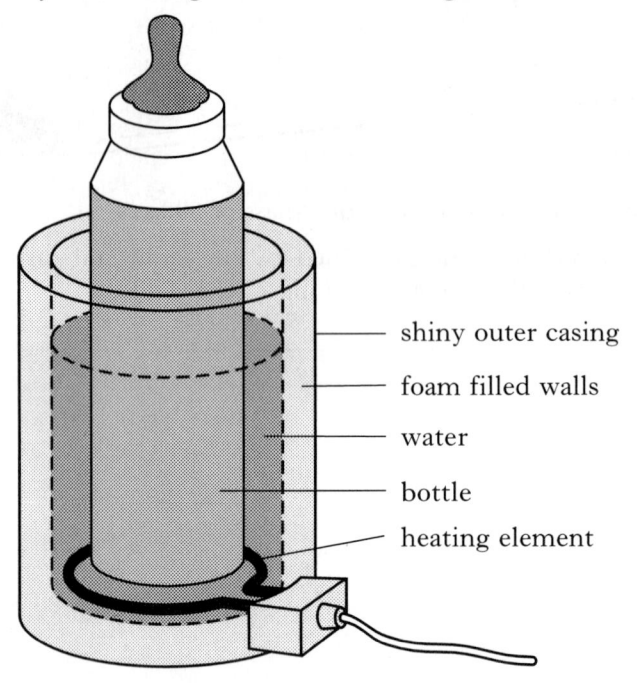

Heat to the warmer is provided by a 100 W heating element. The heating element raises the temperature of the water in the warmer to 40 °C.

(a) State the difference between the terms **heat** and **temperature**.

....

....

.... (2)

(b) Explain why the rate of loss of heat from the bottle warmer is reduced by:

  (i) the foam filled walls;

  ....

  .... (1)

  (ii) the shiny outer casing.

  ....

  .... (1)

(c) The warmer contains 0·5 kg of water at a temperature of 25 °C. The warmer is set to switch off when the water reaches a temperature of 40 °C.

When there is no bottle in the warmer, calculate the minimum time taken to raise the temperature of the water to 40 °C.

(Specific heat capacity of water = 4180 J/kg °C)

Space for working and answer

(3)

(d) When a bottle of milk is placed in the warmer the time taken to reach 40 °C is much longer than the value calculated in part (c).

Give a reason why the time is much longer although the initial temperature and the mass of the water remain the same.

....

.... (1)

12. A shop hires out transformers for use with appliances which are designed to run from 110 V supplies. The table below lists the maximum power output of transformers P, Q, R and S which are available for hire.

Transformer	Maximum power output from transformer in kW
P	0·5
Q	1·1
R	1·5
S	3·0

All the transformers are designed to give a 110 V secondary output when the primary is connected to a 240 V supply.

(a) A person hires one of the transformers to operate a 110 V electric drill. The primary of the transformer is connected to a 240 V supply and the electric drill to the 110 V secondary output. The current in the drill is 18 A.

   (i) Calculate the power of the drill.

   Space for working and answer (2)

   (ii) Which transformer was used to operate the drill?

   .... (1)

(b) The primary coil of each transformer has 1200 turns.

   How many turns has each secondary coil?

   Space for working and answer (2)

(c) (i) When the drill is used the primary of the transformer draws a current of 11 A from the 240 V supply.

Calculate the efficiency of the transformer.

Space for working and answer

(3)

(ii) State **one** reason why transformers are not 100% efficient.

.... (1)

13. The following extracts are taken from a record of the Apollo 11 mission which resulted in the first Moon landing in 1969.

Wednesday 16 July

3.15 am   Astronauts Armstrong, Aldrin and Collins put on their space suits

8.32 am   The rocket lifts off from Kennedy Space Centre

8.35 am   Speed of rocket 10 000 km/h

8.41 am   Speed of rocket 25 000 km/h

(a) On the diagram above, label the forces acting on the rocket at lift off. (1)

(b) Explain, in terms of the forces you have labelled in part (a), why the rocket was able to lift off.

....

.... (1)

(c) Calculate the acceleration, in **km/h/s**, of the rocket in the six minutes between 8.35 am and 8.41 am on Wednesday 16 July 1969.

Space for working and answer

(2)

(d) Each astronaut wore a spacesuit of mass 83 kg.

Calculate the weight of the spacesuit on the Moon.

Space for working and answer

(2)

(e) Why does a spacecraft experience an increase in temperature on re-entry into the atmosphere?

.... (1)

[END OF QUESTION PAPER]

SCOTTISH CERTIFICATE OF EDUCATION 1997

THURSDAY, 15 MAY
1.00 PM – 2.45 PM

PHYSICS
STANDARD GRADE
Credit Level

Marks

1. The tuning dial on a radio displays three different bands which are labelled frequency modulation (FM), medium wave (MW) and long wave (LW). The frequency range for each band is shown below.

Band	Frequency range
FM	88–108 MHz
MW	540–1600 kHz
LW	150–270 kHz

(a) The radio receives a signal with a wavelength of 1190 m.

To which of the above bands is the radio tuned?

You **must** show clearly the calculation used to reach your conclusion.

Space for working and answer

(3)

(b) Signals cannot be received from one of the bands when this radio is used in a village which lies in a deep valley surrounded by hills.

(i) Explain which band is not received.

....

....

....

.... **(2)**

(ii) Houses in the village are unable to receive programmes from the local TV station but can receive satellite TV programmes broadcast on similar frequencies.

Suggest an explanation for this.

....

....

....

.... **(2)**

2. The telecommunication system linking two towns uses copper wire. This system is being replaced by one which uses glass optical fibre.

(a) Give **two** advantages of the glass optical fibre system compared to the copper wire system.

(1) ....

(2) .... **(2)**

(b) A telephone engineer tests the time taken for signals to travel through each system. The distance travelled is the same in each case.

Explain which signal takes the shorter time.

....

.... **(2)**

(c) The engineer sends three test signals X, Y and Z through the new system. An oscilloscope displays the test signals as shown in the diagrams below.

Test signal X   Test signal Y   Test signal Z

The settings on the controls of the oscilloscope are the same for each signal.

Test signal X has a frequency of 2·0 kHz and a peak voltage of 0·5 V.

(i) What is the frequency of test signal Y?

.... **(1)**

(ii) What is the peak voltage of test signal Z?

.... **(1)**

3. The electrical system in a bathroom consists of a motor in an extractor fan and two identical 60 W filament lamps connected to a 230 V supply. These are wired as shown in the circuit diagram below.

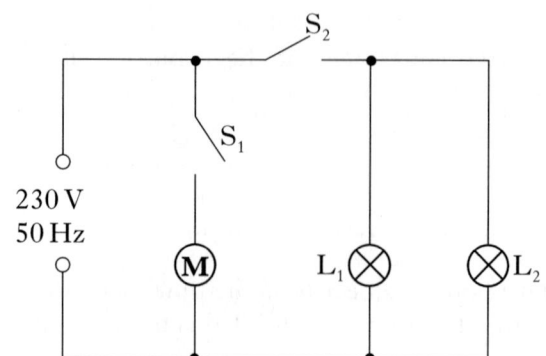

The switches may be open or closed.

(a) Complete the table below, stating whether each of the motor and lamps will be ON or OFF.

Switch S_1	Switch S_2	Motor	Lamp L_1	Lamp L_2
Open	Open			
Open	Closed			
Closed	Open			
Closed	Closed			

(2)

(b) Show, by calculation, that one lamp has a resistance of 882 Ω.

Space for working and answer

(3)

(c) The motor has a resistance of 400 Ω.

Calculate the resistance of the bathroom circuit when the motor and both lamps are switched on.

Space for working and answer

(2)

4. A technician measures the voltage across a component in a circuit using first a digital voltmeter and then an oscilloscope.

Figure 1 shows a digital voltmeter connected to the component and figure 2 shows an oscilloscope connected to the same component.

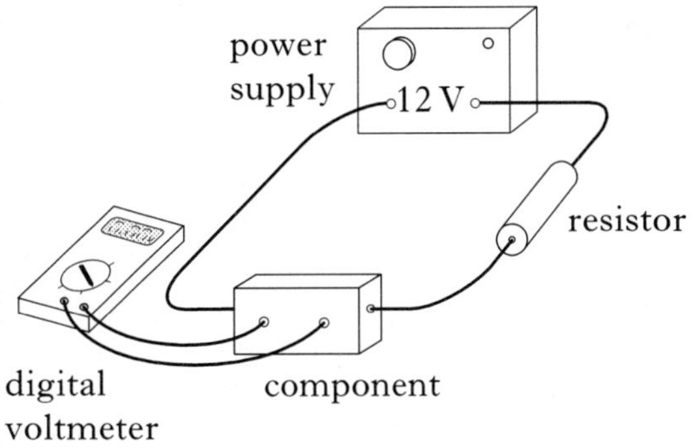

figure 1

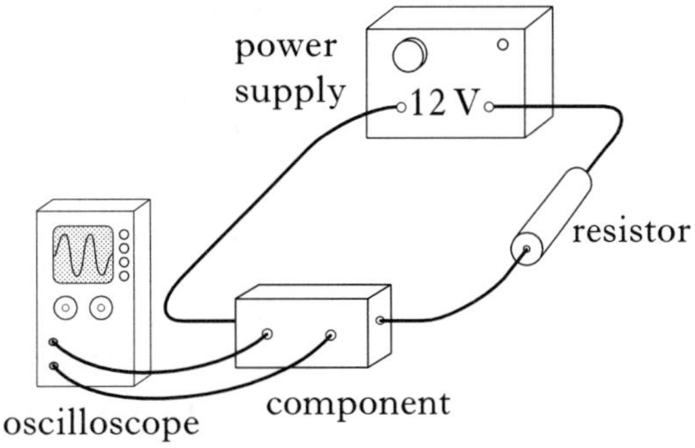

figure 2

(a) State whether the voltage across the component is direct or alternating.

.... (1)

(b) The graph below shows how the voltage across the component varies with time.

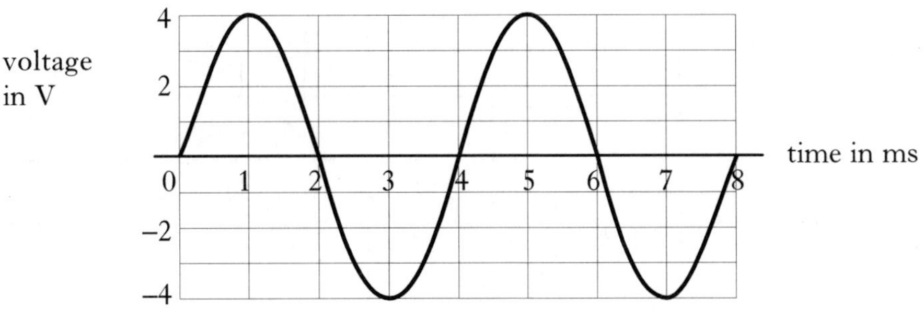

What is the peak voltage across the component?

.... (1)

(c) How does the peak voltage compare with the voltage reading which would be shown on the digital voltmeter?

.... (1)

5. A filament lamp is connected in a circuit as shown below.

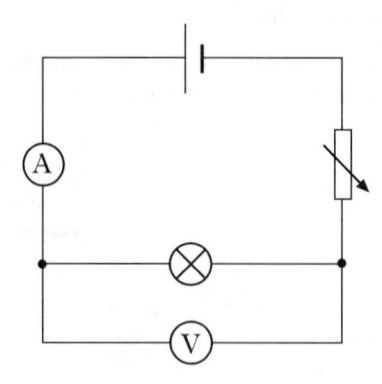

The current in the lamp is altered. The voltage across the lamp is measured. The graph below shows how the voltage varies with the current for several values of current.

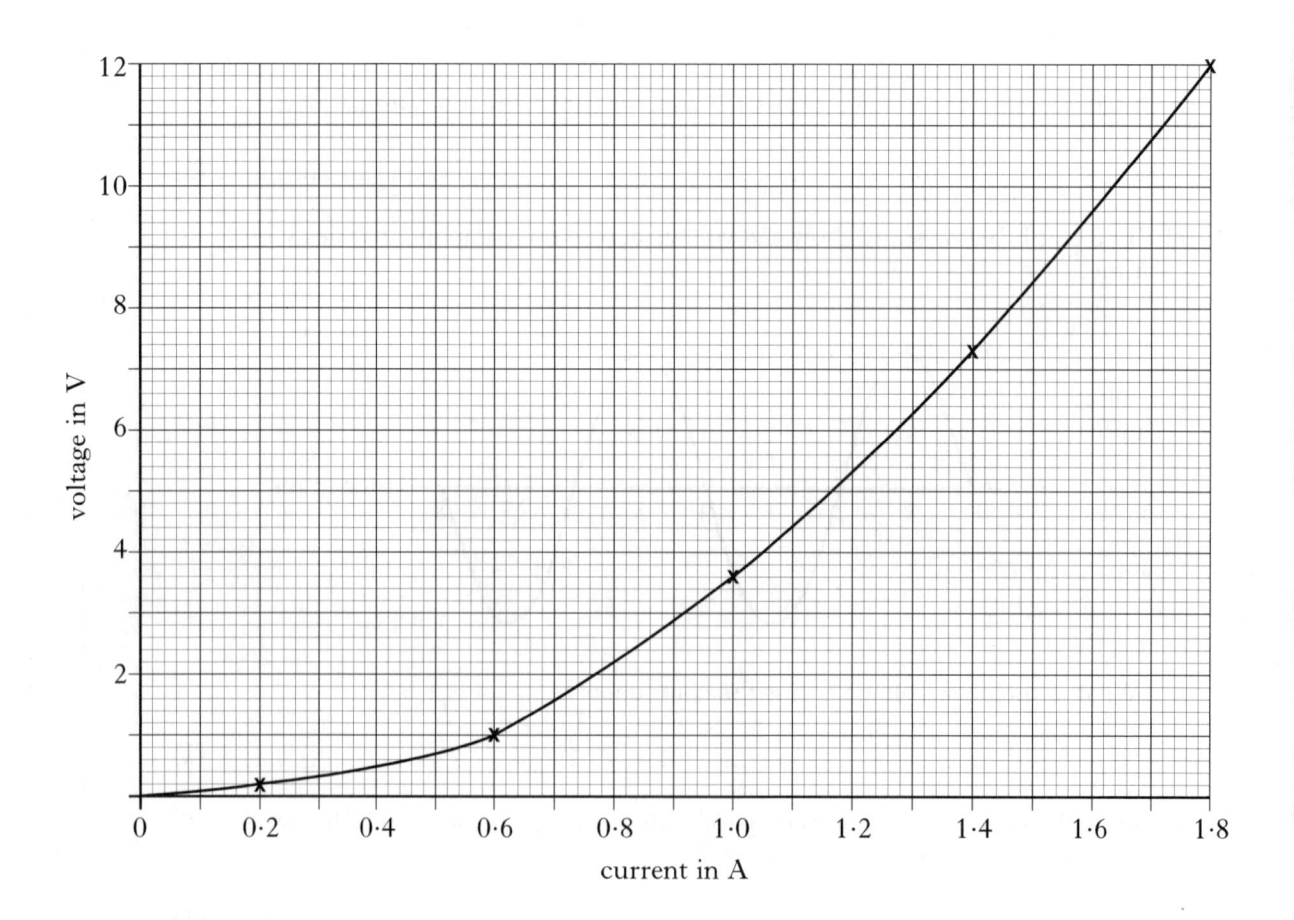

(a) State what happens to the resistance of the lamp as the current is increased. You **must** justify your answer by using information from the graph.

Space for working and answer

(3)

(b) The manufacturer states that the lamp has a power rating of 24 W when operating at 12 V.

Determine whether the power rating of this lamp is the same as that quoted by the manufacturer. You **must** clearly show the working which leads you to your answer.

Space for working and answer

(3)

6. (*a*) The diagram shows rays of light from a distant object reaching the eye of a person with normal sight. The focusing of the light is achieved by a combination of the cornea and the lens.

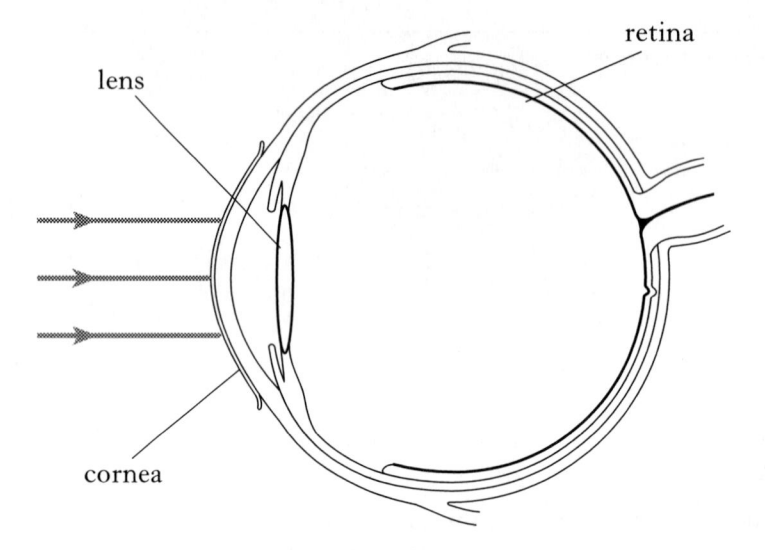

(i) Complete the diagram above to show the path of rays of light within the eye. **(2)**

(ii) This combination of cornea and lens has a power of + 59 D.

Calculate the focal length of the combination.

Space for working and answer

(2)

(b) Alison wears spectacles for reading and decides to measure the focal length of one of her spectacle lenses. She sets up a screen, a brightly lit bulb and a metre stick as shown in the diagram below.

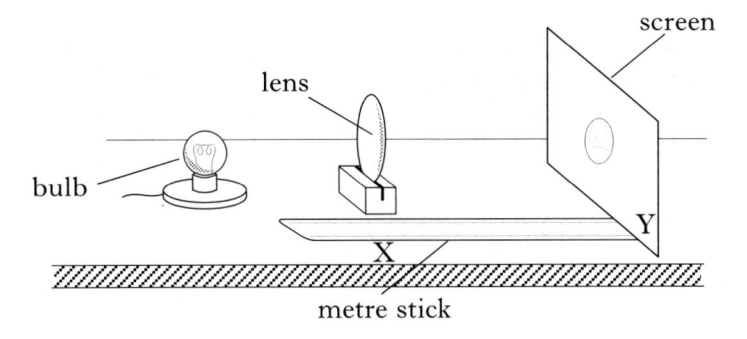

Alison moves the screen until a clear image of the bulb is obtained and then measures the distance XY between the lens and the screen.

(i) Give a reason why the distance XY is not equal to the focal length of the lens.

.... (1)

(ii) State the change Alison should make in carrying out her experiment so that she measures the focal length of the lens.

....

.... (1)

(c) Alison's grandfather has used two pairs of spectacles for several years. One pair was for distance vision and the other for close work. The optician replaces the two pairs with one pair having lenses which are in two parts as shown below.

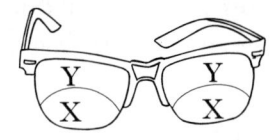

The parts of the lenses have power of +2D and +4D.

Part X is for close work and part Y is for distance vision.

Complete the table below to indicate the power of each part.

Lens part	Power
X	
Y	

(1)

7. (a) A hospital uses radioactive Technetium in the diagnosis of tumours. The Technetium is injected into the patient.

The label on a sample which is delivered to the hospital is shown below.

TECHNETIUM	
Date of delivery	15/5/1997
Time of delivery	1.00 p.m.
Half-life	6 hours
Activity on delivery	600 MBq
Type of radiation	Gamma

(i) What is meant by the term "half-life"?

....

.... **(1)**

(ii) Why is a sample with a short half-life used in diagnosis?

....

.... **(1)**

(iii) If the sample of Technetium is not used, the hospital is allowed to dispose of it. This is permitted once its activity has fallen below 75 MBq.

Show, by calculation, the date and time when the sample will be ready for disposal.

Space for working and answer

(3)

(b) The effect of radiation absorbed by living materials depends on a number of factors.

Name **two** of the factors.

(1) ....

(2) .... **(2)**

(c) Members of the hospital staff wear film badges to monitor any radiation to which they may be exposed.

The film is contained in a plastic holder with windows of different materials as shown in the diagram. The whole badge is protected from light.

- open window (no material covering)
- plastic 0·1 mm thickness
- aluminium 3 mm thickness
- lead 1 mm thickness

(i) Shade the window or windows on the diagram above where the film will be affected if the wearer is accidentally exposed to the radiation from the Technetium source. **(1)**

(ii) Describe how the badge is used to indicate how much radiation has been received.

....

....

.... **(1)**

1997

8. Figure 1 shows a conveyor belt in a supermarket. The belt is driven by a motor.

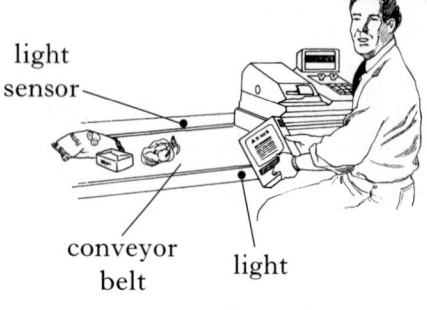

figure 1

Part of the mechanism which operates the motor uses a light-sensitive switch.

The conveyor belt stops when a package comes between the light and the light sensor.

(a) The light-sensitive part of the system is shown in figure 2.

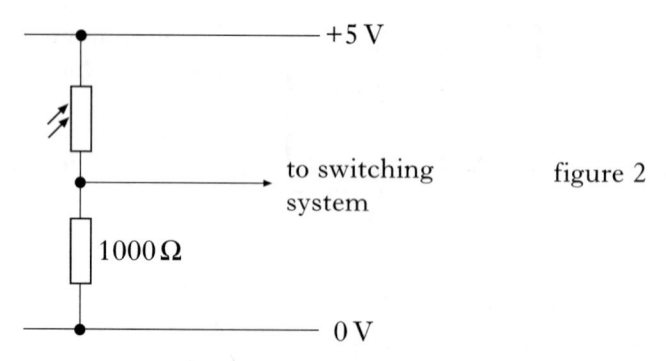

figure 2

The resistance of the light dependent resistor (LDR) in different lighting conditions is shown in the table below.

Lighting condition	Resistance of LDR
Light	100 Ω
Dark	10 000 Ω

Calculate the voltage across the 1000 Ω resistor when the LDR is in darkness.

Space for working and answer

(2)

(b) The conveyor belt motor is connected to the light sensor using a transistor and relay as shown in figure 3.

The transistor switches off when the voltage across the 1000 Ω resistor drops below 0·7 V. The relay switch is used to switch the motor on and off.

figure 3

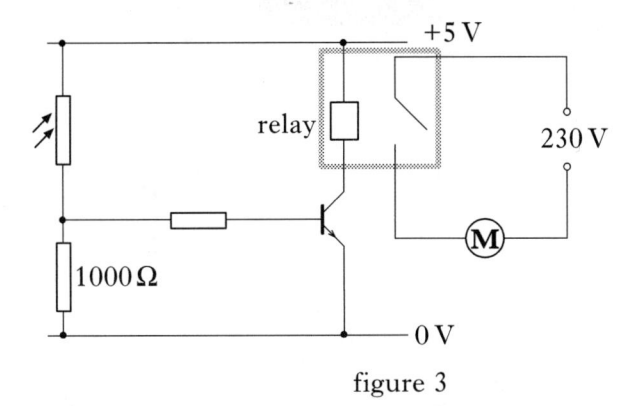

Figure 4 shows the construction of the relay switch.

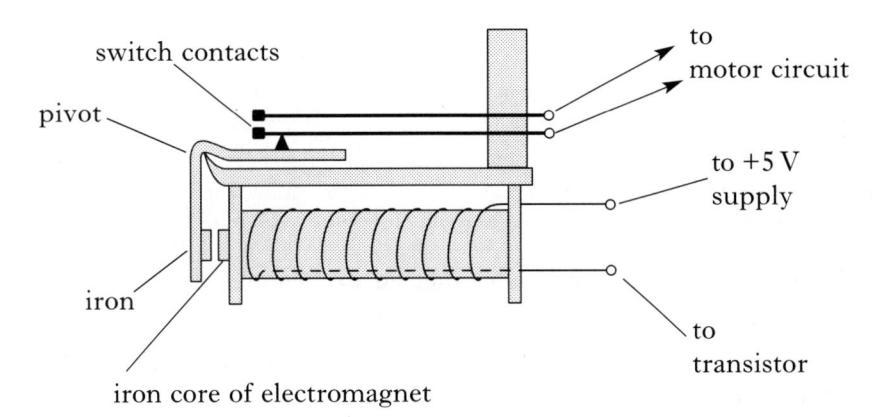

figure 4

Explain why the conveyor belt stops when a package comes between the light and the light sensor.

....

....

....

....

.... (3)

9. The timer in a microwave oven uses a circuit which produces pulses. The part of the circuit which generates the pulses is shown below. The voltage supply has not been included in the diagram.

(a) Complete the table below to show the logic levels at X and Y when the capacitor in the circuit is charged and when it is uncharged.

	Logic level at X	Logic level at Y
Capacitor charged		
Capacitor uncharged		

(2)

(b) The output from the above circuit is connected to a counter and a seven segment display.

At what frequency should the pulses be generated for the seven segment display to change every second?

.... (1)

(c) When tested, the timer was found to run slowly.

What change should be made to the circuit to correct this fault? Explain your answer.

....

.... (2)

10. Two factors which contribute to road safety are:

(1) leaving a suitable distance between vehicles;

(2) using safety belts.

(*a*) Some motorists drive too close to the car in front on motorways. In an experiment, large arrows are painted 24 m apart on a road in an attempt to improve safety.

The advice to motorists travelling at the maximum speed of 70 mph is *"make sure that you can see at least three arrows between your car and the car in front"*.

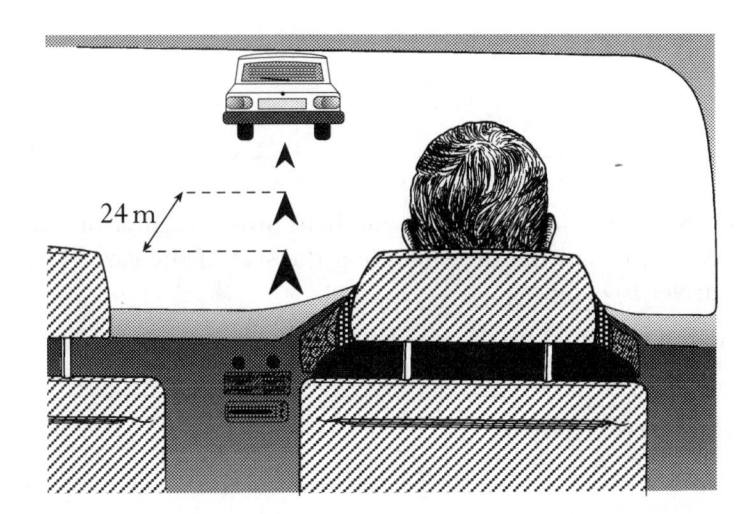

(i) A car took 0·8 s to travel from one arrow to the next.

Calculate the average speed of the car between the arrows.

Space for working and answer

(2)

(ii) Road safety experts extend the experiment to built up areas with a speed limit of 30 mph.

How would the distance between the arrows on such a road compare with that on the motorway where the speed limit is 70 mph?

.... (1)

(b) (i) A car travelling at a speed of 30 m/s approaches slow moving traffic. The car decelerates at 4·5 m/s² for a time of 5 s.

Calculate the speed of the car on reaching the slow moving traffic.

Space for working and answer

(2)

(ii) During the above deceleration, the seat belt provides 50% of the force required to prevent the driver leaving the seat of the car. The mass of the driver is 72 kg.

Calculate the force exerted by the seat belt on the driver.

Space for working and answer

(3)

11. Contestants in a competition shown on TV have to go round an assault course. On one of the obstacles they climb rope netting and then drop down the other side. The height of the netting is 6·0 m above the ground.

A contestant of mass 65 kg climbs the netting. After stepping over the edge at P, the contestant falls **freely** for 0·7 s before making contact with a slide at Q. From Q the contestant slows down and comes to rest at R.

(a) The 65 kg contestant climbs the netting from the ground to P.

Calculate the gravitational potential energy gained by the contestant.

Space for working and answer

(2)

(b) The contestant falls freely (ie without friction) between P and Q.

(i) Name the force acting on the contestant between P and Q.

.... (1)

(ii) Calculate the size of the force on the contestant between P and Q.

Space for working and answer

(2)

(c) Using the axes given below, draw the speed-time graph for the fall from P to Q.

Space for working

(2)

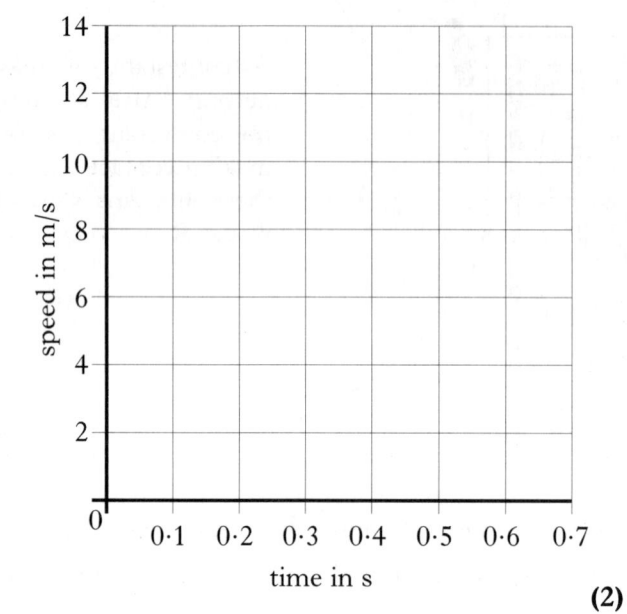

(d) Calculate the height of point Q above R.

Space for working and answer

(3)

12. Figure 1 shows a dynamo fitted to a bicycle. Figure 2 shows how the dynamo is constructed.

bicycle wheel

figure 1

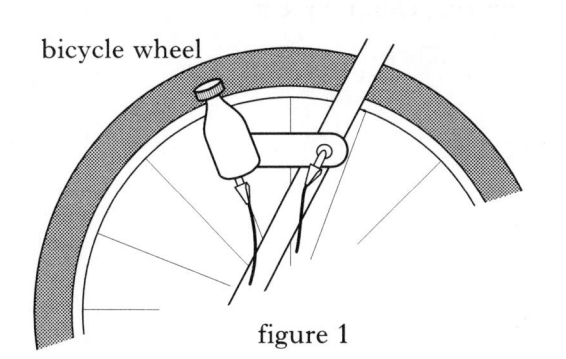

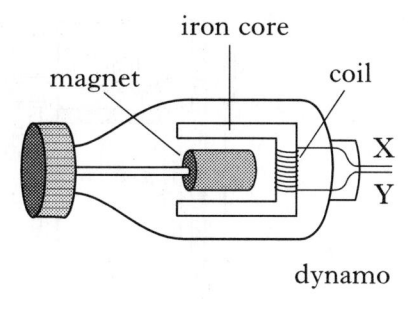

iron core
magnet
coil
X
Y
dynamo

figure 2

The bicycle is pedalled along a level road at a steady speed and a voltage is produced across XY.

(a) Explain why a voltage is produced across XY.

....

....

.... **(2)**

(b) The diagram below shows how the output voltage from the dynamo varies with time when the pedals are turned at a steady speed.

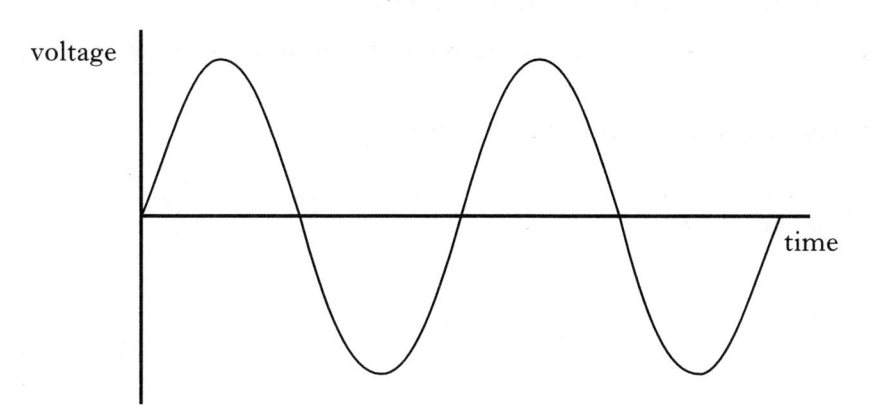

On the diagram above, sketch a curve which would be obtained if the bicycle was pedalled at a **slower** steady speed. **(2)**

13. The diagram below shows part of a refrigerator which has a freezing compartment.

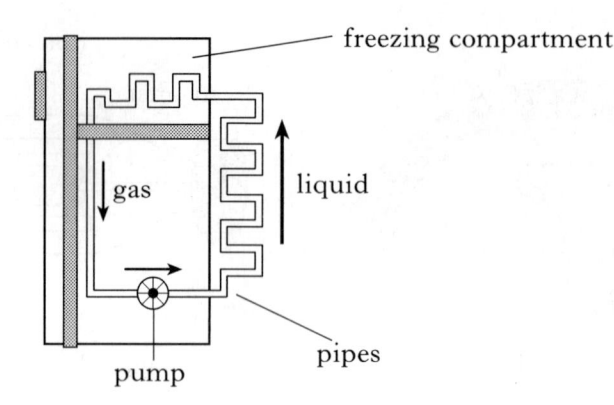

(a) A substance which is called a coolant is circulated in the pipes by the pump.

(i) Name the change in state of the coolant in the freezing compartment.

.... **(1)**

(ii) Explain why this change of state keeps the freezer compartment cool.

.... **(1)**

(b) An ice tray containing 0·2 kg of water is placed in the freezing compartment. The water cools to 0 °C and then freezes.

Calculate how much heat is given out as the water in the tray freezes at 0 °C.

[Specific latent heat of fusion of water = $3·34 \times 10^5$ J/kg]

Space for working and answer

(2)

14. A mobile telephone operates using rechargeable batteries. When not in use the batteries are recharged using a base unit. The base unit is connected to a 230 V a.c. supply using a transformer.

The rating plate on the transformer is shown below.

> For overnight charges only
> OUTPUT: 24 V   4·6 W
> SPD 6204
> INPUT: 230 V   50 Hz   A.C. ONLY
> □   MADE IN UK PX 450

(a) The primary coil of the transformer has 690 turns.

Calculate the number of turns on the secondary coil of the transformer.

Space for working and answer (2)

(b) Calculate the current drawn from the supply if the transformer is 100% efficient.

Space for working and answer (2)

(c) In practice, the transformer is not 100% efficient.

Give a reason for this.

.... (1)

15. In deep space, a spaceship of mass 16 000 kg is trying to dock with a space station. The spaceship is stationary.

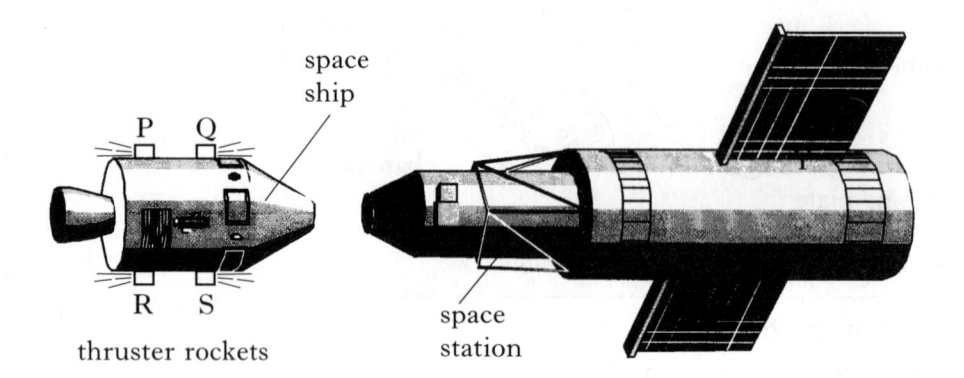

The spaceship has four small thruster rockets P, Q, R and S as shown, which are used when docking. In order to approach the space station, the crew of the spaceship fire two of the thruster rockets for 10 seconds and then switch them off. After 10 seconds the speed of the spaceship is 2 m/s.

(a) Calculate the gain in the kinetic energy of the spaceship after the 10 seconds.

Space for working and answer

(2)

(b) Describe and explain the motion of the spaceship **after** the motors are switched off.

....
....
.... (2)

(c) Describe what the crew must do to bring the spaceship back to rest.

....
....
.... (2)

16. On one of the missions to the Moon, astronauts took a large mirror which they set up and left behind on the surface. Scientists on Earth determined the distance between the Earth and the Moon by reflecting laser light from the mirror.

(a) The astronauts found it easier to lift the mirror on the Moon than on the Earth.

Suggest a reason for this. You must quote figures from the data sheet to support your answer.

....

.... **(2)**

(b) Using a powerful laser and a clock, scientists on Earth measured the exact time for the laser light to travel to the Moon and back. The reading on the clock was 2·56 s.

[Speed of light in air or vacuum = 3×10^8 m/s]

Calculate the distance from the Earth to the Moon.

Space for working and answer

(3)

(c) While setting up the mirror on the Moon, the astronauts were in radio communication with Earth.

How did the time taken for the radio waves to travel to the Moon compare with the time taken for the laser light to travel to the Moon?

.... **(1)**

(d) Visible light from the laser is one part of the electromagnetic spectrum. The diagram below shows the electromagnetic spectrum but two parts, P and Q are missing.

R	Radio and TV
	P
	Q
	Visible light	S
	Ultraviolet
	X-rays
	Gamma radiation

(i) Name radiation P and radiation Q.

Radiation P ....

Radiation Q .... **(1)**

(ii) Which of the arrows, R or S, shows the direction of increasing wavelength of the electromagnetic radiation in the spectrum?

.... **(1)**

[END OF QUESTION PAPER]

SCOTTISH CERTIFICATE OF EDUCATION
1998

FRIDAY, 15 MAY
10.45 AM – 12.30 PM

PHYSICS
STANDARD GRADE
Credit Level

Marks

1. Information may be passed between a telephone exchange and a receiver in a number of ways.

    (a) Electrical signals from the telephone exchange are converted to light signals. The light signals are then transmitted through an optical fibre to the receiver.

    Complete the diagram in figure 1 to show the path of a ray of light as it passes along the optical fibre.

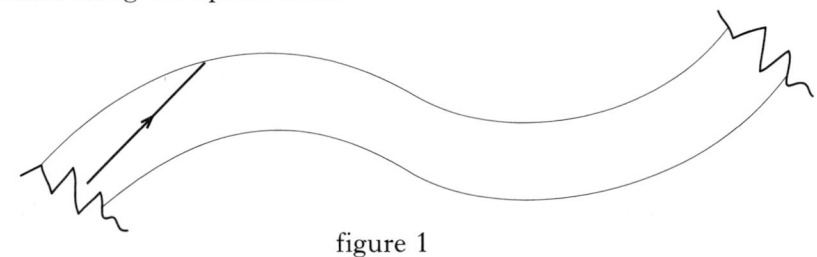

    figure 1 (1)

    (b) Electrical signals from the telephone exchange are converted to microwaves. The microwaves are transmitted via a satellite to the receiver as shown in figure 2.

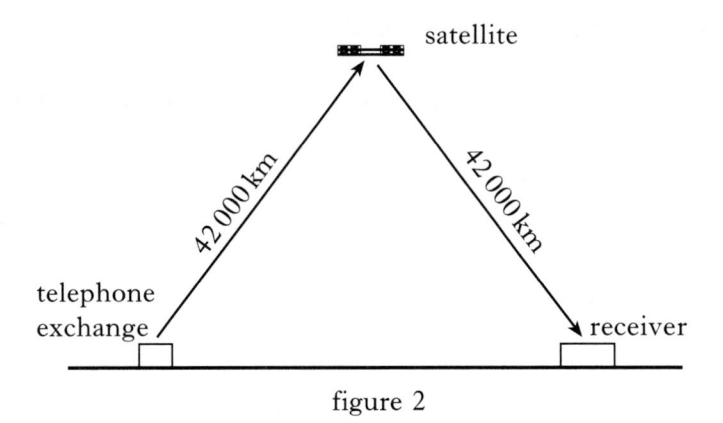

    figure 2

    Calculate the time taken for the microwave signal to travel from the telephone exchange to the receiver.

    Space for working and answer

    (3)

2. (a) Firefighters use special viewers which detect radiations from the part of the electromagnetic spectrum marked Q in figure 1.

Gamma rays	X-rays	P	Visible	Q	Micro-waves	TV	Radio

figure 1

(i) Name radiation Q.

.... (1)

(ii) Describe how the viewer is able to detect an unconscious person in a dark, smoke-filled room.

....

....

.... (1)

(b) The display screen on the viewer produces a black and white picture.

A pupil suggests that it would be better to produce a colour picture on the screen using a system of phosphor dots which can emit red, green or blue light.

Which dots would glow to produce cyan on the display screen?

.... (1)

3. An electric shower unit is supplied with cold water at a temperature of 16 °C as shown below. An electric heater in the unit is used to increase the temperature of the water so that it comes out of the shower at 40 °C. The shower provides 5 kg of hot water every minute.

hot water out—40 °C

electric heater

cold water in—16 °C

(a) Calculate the heat energy supplied to the water every minute.
   [specific heat capacity of water = 4180 J/kg °C]

   Space for working and answer (2)

(b) Calculate the power output of the heater **in watts**.

   Space for working and answer (2)

(c) The manufacturer of the shower states that the flow rate may have to be adjusted in winter if a hot water temperature of 40 °C is to be maintained.

   Explain whether the flow rate would be greater or less than 5 kg per minute.

   ....

   .... (2)

4. A car starter motor is operated when the driver closes the ignition switch.

Figure 1 shows the system used to operate the starter motor.

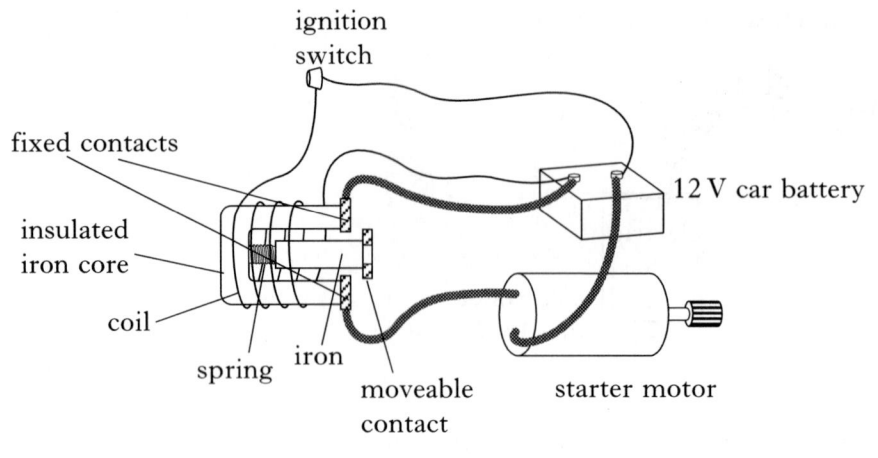

figure 1

(a) Explain why closing the ignition switch makes the starter motor operate.

....

....

....

.... (3)

(b) The voltage across the cable connecting the battery to the starter motor is 0·25 V when the current in the cable is 400 A. The cable has a resistance of 5×10^{-4} ohm per metre.

Calculate the length of this cable.

Space for working and answer

(3)

Marks | K&U | PS

(*c*) A diagram of the starter motor is shown in figure 2.

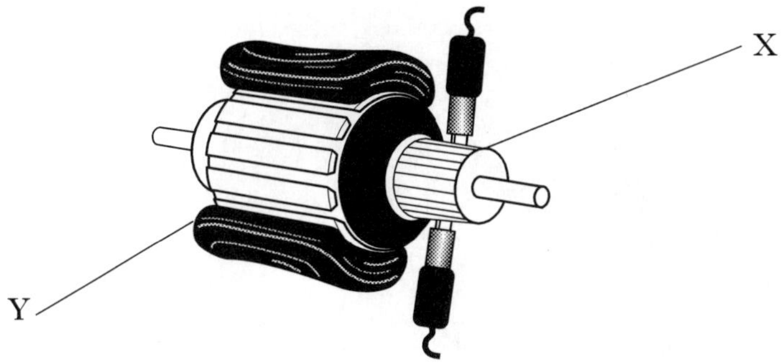

figure 2

Name the parts labelled X and Y on the diagram.

X .... Y .... **(1)**

(*d*) When the starter motor operates, a charge of 360 C is drawn from the battery.

How long will it take to recharge the battery if a charging current of 5 A is used?

Space for working and answer

(2)

5. An illuminated food cabinet, used in a canteen, has warm and hot areas as shown in figure 1. Separate heating elements provide heat for the warm and hot areas.

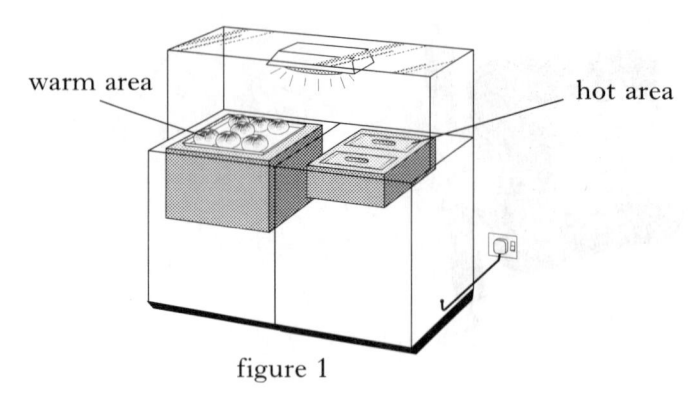

figure 1

The heating elements and lamp are connected to the 230 V mains supply as shown in figure 2. The resistance of each heating element and the lamp is indicated in figure 2.

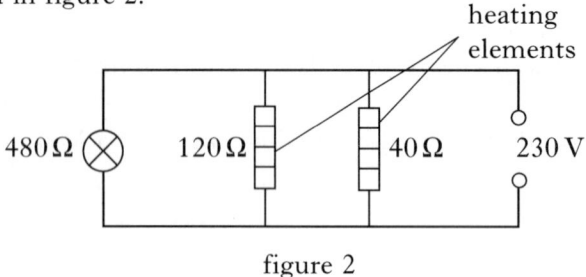

figure 2

(a) Calculate the power of the lamp.

Space for working and answer

(2)

(b) Calculate the combined resistance of the lamp and the heating elements.

Space for working and answer

(2)

(c) Calculate the current drawn from the supply when the cabinet is operating.

Space for working and answer

(2)

6. A motorist has to wear spectacles to read the number plate on a car which is 20 m away. However, the information on the instrument panel in a car can be read easily by the motorist without wearing spectacles.

(a) Explain whether the spectacle lenses are convex or concave.

(*You may draw diagrams to illustrate your answer if you wish.*)

Space for answer

(3)

(b) The focal length of one of the spectacle lenses is 67 cm.
Calculate the power of the lens.

Space for working and answer

(2)

7. Read the following passage about eye protection.

Certain groups of people may be exposed to high levels of ultraviolet light. Their eyes must be protected. Spectacle lenses can be treated with special coatings to give protection.

Scientists who regularly use illuminated microscopes must use protective spectacles. These must allow the maximum transmission of visible light but protect against ultraviolet light.

People taking part in winter sports also require spectacles to protect their eyes from ultraviolet light. The spectacles also cut down light received from the sun and reflected from the snow.

The graphs P, Q, R and S below provide information on spectacle lenses with four different coatings.

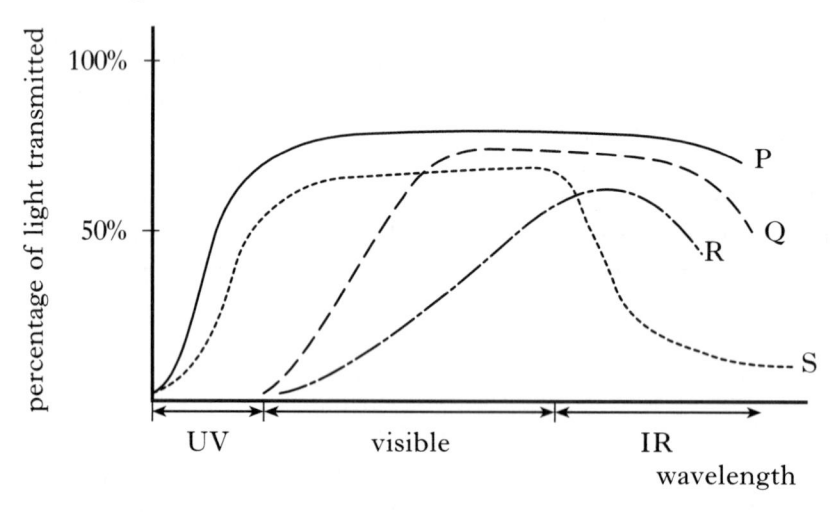

(a) Which spectacle lens should be used by scientists using illuminated microscopes? Give a reason for your answer.

....

....

.... (2)

(b) Which spectacle lens should be used by people taking part in winter sports? Give a reason for your answer.

....

....

.... (2)

8. Doctors use radioactive technetium to investigate different parts of the human body. A solution of technetium is injected into the body and a gamma camera is used to detect the radiation emitted.

(a) The half-life of technetium is 6 hours.

What is meant by the term "half-life"?

....

....

.... (1)

(b) The table below indicates the minimum activity of the technetium solutions which are used to investigate various parts of the body.

Part of body to be investigated	Minimum activity of solution (MBq)
Brain	800
Lungs	80
Liver	200
Thyroid	40

A solution is made up with 800 MBq of technetium at 8 am.

(i) What is the latest possible time that the solution could be used for investigating a patient's liver?

Space for working and answer

(2)

(ii) At 10 pm, which part or parts of the body listed in the table could still be investigated using the solution? Explain your answer.

....

.... (3)

(c) The third column in the table below lists values which give a measure of the biological effect of the radiation on the absorbing tissue.

Part of body to be investigated	Minimum activity of solution (MBq)	.... (....................)
Brain	800	0·0170
Lungs	80	0·0003
Liver	200	0·0027
Thyroid	40	0·0020

Complete the table by adding the name and unit of the quantity whose value is listed in the third column.

(2)

9. A pupil is asked to devise a circuit which will switch on automatically a light emitting diode (LED) when a room becomes dark.

Part of the circuit the pupil sets up is shown in the diagram below.

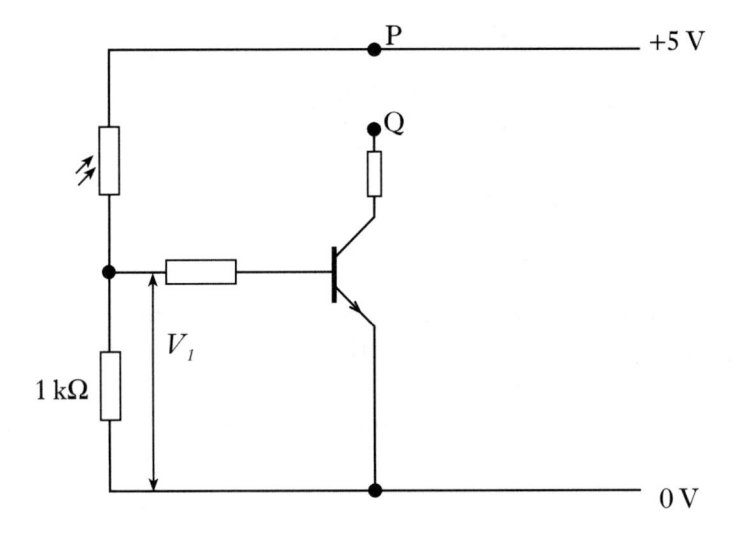

(a) Complete the circuit diagram above to show a LED correctly connected between P and Q. **(1)**

(b) The properties of the light dependent resistor (LDR) in the circuit used by the pupil are shown in the table below.

Lighting conditions	Resistance of LDR
Bright	100 Ω
Dark	10 kΩ

V_1 is the input voltage to the transistor. The transistor switches on fully when V_1 rises above 0·7 V.

(i) Calculate the value of the input voltage V_1 in dark conditions.

(Use an appropriate number of figures in your answer.)

Space for working and answer

(3)

(ii) When the room is dark and the LED is correctly connected, it will **not** light. Explain.

....

....

....

.... **(2)**

(c) Using only the components shown in the circuit diagram, state one change which should be made to the circuit to make it operate properly.

.... **(1)**

10. A driverless train is operated by sending voltage pulses of different frequency along the railway track to a motor control in the train. The different frequencies of pulse that are used to give different instructions to the motor control of the train are represented by the pulse pattern in the table below.

Instruction to motor control	Pulse pattern
Start train	4 pulses in 1·0 s, voltage 5 V
Travel at constant speed	10 pulses in 1·0 s, voltage 5 V
Stop train	no pulses

(a) State the frequency of the pulses used to start the train.

.... (1)

(b) The pulses are produced by the pulse generator shown in figure 1. The supply voltage is not shown.

figure 1

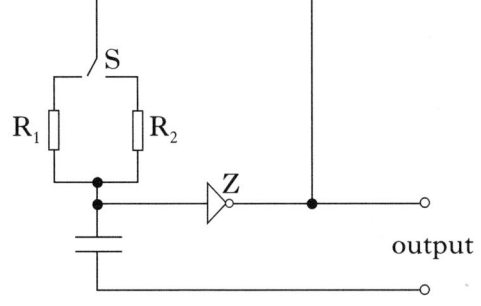

(i) Name component Z.

.... (1)

(ii) Switch S makes a connection with resistor R_1 to start the train and with resistor R_2 to run the train at constant speed.
Which of the resistors has the lower resistance? Give a reason for your answer.

....

.... (2)

(c) The train cannot start until its doors are closed. An electronic circuit is used to give an output which shows whether a door of the train is open or closed.

The circuit gives an output of +5 V (logic 1) when the door is closed and an output of 0 V (logic 0) when the door is open. Two circuits P and Q are shown in figure 2. Switch S is closed when the train door is closed.

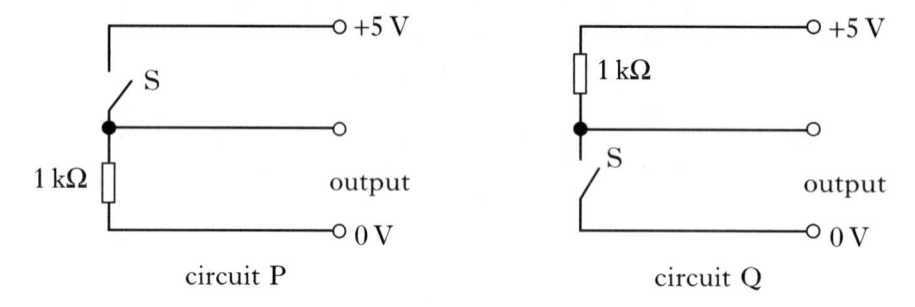

figure 2

State which of the circuits P or Q is used and give a reason for your answer.

....

....

.... (2)

11. A roller coaster is designed with a vertical drop as shown below. A vehicle is moved from P to the top of a slope at Q. At the top of the slope the vehicle is released and it falls vertically from R to S.

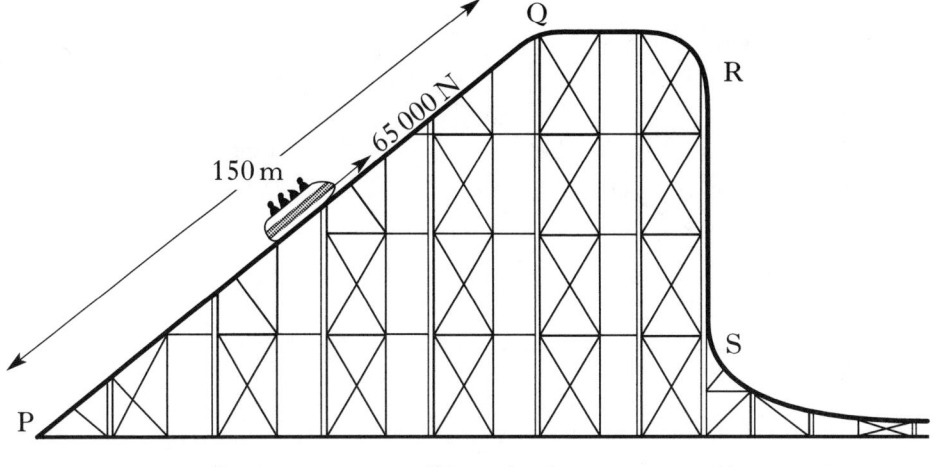

figure 1

(a) A force of 65 000 N is applied over a distance of 150 m to move the vehicle at a constant speed from P to Q.

How much work is done by the force in moving the vehicle?

Space for working and answer

(2)

(b) The vehicle and passengers reach a maximum height of 110 m. The total mass of vehicle and passengers is 8500 kg.

Calculate the potential energy gained by the vehicle and passengers.

Space for working and answer

(2)

(c) The vehicle is designed to travel at 5 m/s at R and to travel vertically for 4 s to S. A pupil draws a speed–time graph of the motion between R and S as shown in figure 2.

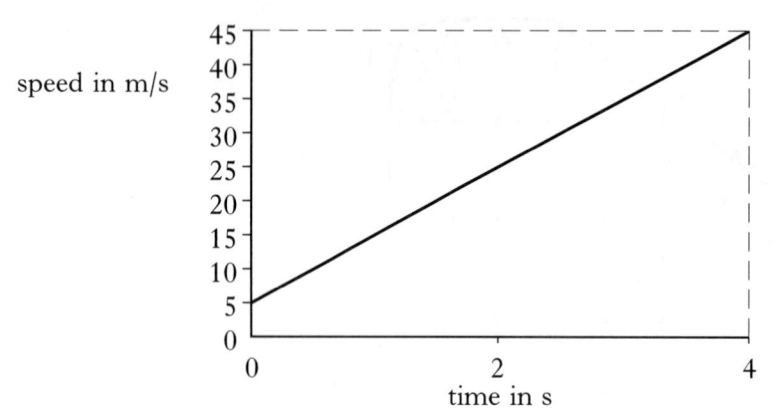

figure 2

Calculate the value the pupil's speed-time graph predicts for the length of the vertical drop from R to S.

Space for working and answer

(2)

(d) In drawing the speed-time graph, the pupil has assumed that the acceleration of the vehicle is 10 m/s^2.

Explain whether the actual value for the vertical drop would be greater or less than the value predicted from the pupil's speed-time graph.

....

....

.... (2)

(e) Describe how the speed of the vehicle at S could be measured.

....

....

.... (2)

12. The highway code requires drivers to know about the overall stopping distance for vehicles. The overall stopping distance is made up of:

   (1) the **thinking distance**—the distance travelled while the driver "thinks" about braking;

   (2) the **braking distance**—the distance travelled while braking.

   The following diagram gives information about the overall stopping distance of a car and the time for the car to come to rest under different conditions. Timing starts from the moment the driver recognises there is a need to brake and stops when the car comes to a halt.

	Thinking distance	Braking distance	Overall stopping distance
Car and driver Speed 20 m/s Dry road	14 m	35 m	49 m
Car and driver Speed 20 m/s Wet road	14 m	60 m	74 m
Car and driver plus three passengers Speed 20 m/s Dry road	14 m	47 m	61 m

   Time in s 0   0·7   4·2 5·4   6·7

   (a) Explain why the thinking distance is the same for the different conditions.

   ....

   .... (2)

   (b) Calculate the deceleration of the car on the wet road.

   Space for working and answer

   (2)

(c) The total mass of the car and driver is 1500 kg.

Calculate the unbalanced force on the car while braking on the wet road.

Space for working and answer

(2)

(d) Explain why the stopping distance on a dry road increases when the car has passengers.

....

....

.... (2)

13. Electrical power may be provided to remote homes by a combination of wind and solar generators as shown in the diagram below.

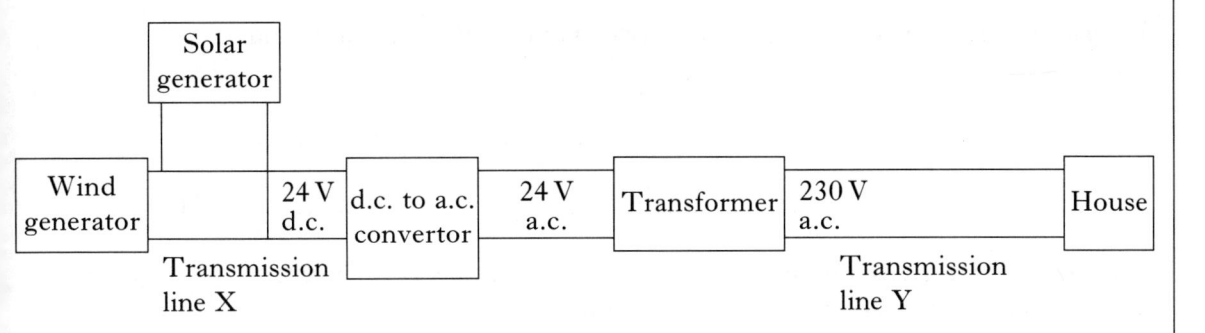

[Diagram: Wind generator → Transmission line X → 24 V d.c. → d.c. to a.c. convertor → 24 V a.c. → Transformer → 230 V a.c. → Transmission line Y → House. Solar generator connects into the 24 V d.c. line.]

(a) The following graphs show how the average wind speed and average daily sunlight vary over a year.

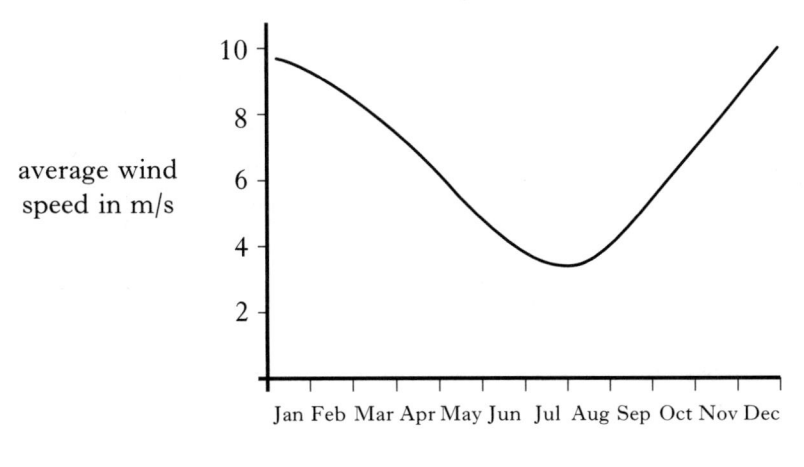

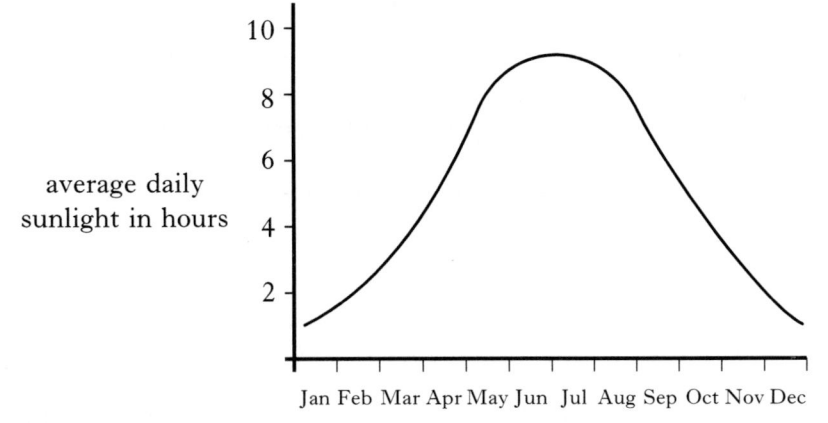

[Graph 1: average wind speed in m/s vs months Jan–Dec. High (~10) in Jan, decreasing to minimum (~3.5) around Jul, rising back to ~10 in Dec.]

[Graph 2: average daily sunlight in hours vs months Jan–Dec. Low (~1) in Jan, peaking (~9) around Jun/Jul, falling back to ~1 in Dec.]

Explain why the combination of wind and solar generators provides an effective system.

....

.... (2)

(b) The output voltage from the solar and wind generators is 24 V d.c.

Explain the need for the d.c. to a.c. convertor between the generators and the transformer.

....

.... **(1)**

(c) The transformer steps up the voltage from 24 V to 230 V. There are 480 turns on the primary coil of the transformer.

Calculate the number of turns on the secondary coil.

Space for working and answer

(2)

(d) The electrical power loss is less in transmission line Y than in transmission line X although the resistance of line Y is greater.

Explain.

....

....

.... **(2)**

14. (a) Figure 1 shows a space shuttle consisting of an orbiter, called *Discovery*, and booster rockets. At lift off *Discovery* and the booster rockets have a total mass of 2.05×10^6 kg and the thrust of the rocket engines is 2.91×10^7 N. The frictional forces acting on the shuttle at lift off are negligible.

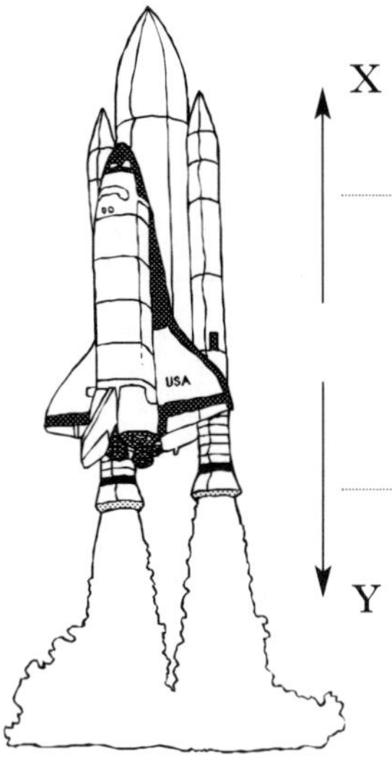

figure 1

At lift off:

(i) label, on figure 1, the two forces X and Y acting on the shuttle in the directions shown; **(1)**

(ii) calculate the weight of the shuttle;

Space for working and answer

(2)

(iii) calculate the acceleration of the shuttle.

Space for working and answer

(3)

(b) The booster rockets are parachuted to Earth before *Discovery* enters orbit around the Earth. In orbit, *Discovery's* rocket engines are switched off. Figure 2 shows *Discovery* in orbit around the Earth.

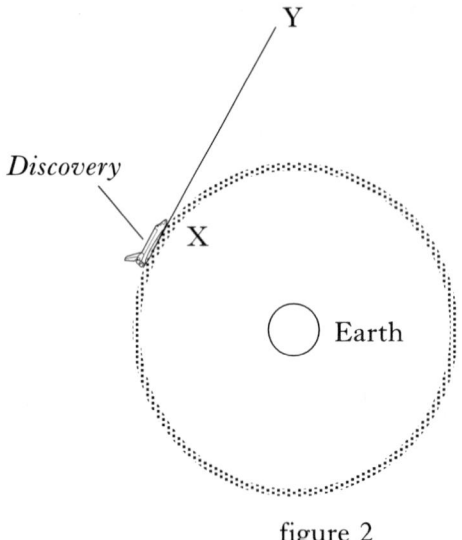

figure 2

Explain why *Discovery* remains in orbit and does not:

(i) move closer to the Earth;

....

....

....

(ii) move off into space along XY.

....

....

.... (2)

15. (a) In 1971, a lunar module carrying two astronauts landed on the Moon's surface. The gravitational field strength on the Moon is different from that on Earth.

   (i) What is meant by "gravitational field strength"?

   ....

   .... **(1)**

   (ii) The gravitational field strength at the surface of the Moon is 1·6 N/kg.

   What is the value of the acceleration due to gravity at the surface of the Moon?

   .... **(1)**

(b) One of the astronauts played golf on the moon. The golf ball was struck horizontally from the edge of a steep crater. It landed 2 seconds later, 25 m away as shown in the diagram below.

(diagram: astronaut striking golf ball horizontally off a crater edge, 25 m horizontal distance)

   (i) Calculate the horizontal speed of the ball after being struck.

   Space for working and answer

   (2)

(ii) Calculate the vertical speed of the ball on landing.

Space for working and answer

(2)

(iii) How would the horizontal distance travelled by a ball projected with the same horizontal speed from the same height on Earth compare with that on the Moon?

Explain your answer.

....

....

....

....

.... (3)

[END OF QUESTION PAPER]

CREDIT PHYSICS ANSWERS — 1994

1. *(a)* Nd-YAG   *(b)* Treatment of damaged muscle   *(c)* 4.76×10^{14} Hz   *(d)* 6 J

2. *(a)*

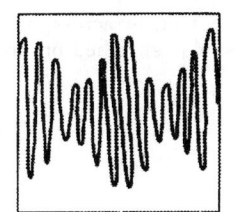

   (b) 3.5×10^{-3} s

   (b) The electron beam in the TV tube scans backwards and forwards across the screen and up and down the screen as shown in the diagram. The scanning beam produces a picture made up of lines. Each line is made up of bits which vary in brightness. When all the lines are built up together a picture is seen on the screen

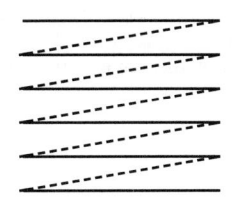

3. *(a)* 60 Ω   *(b)* 60 Ω   *(c)* 960 W
   (d) (i) Resistance
   (ii) The faulty element will not give a reading of 18 Ω or 24 Ω.
   (iii) Open circuit.

4. *(a)* 6 hours
   (b) Gamma rays are used because they can pass through body tissue.
   (c) The images produced have more detail than those provided by a single X-ray.
   (d) (i) Ionisation is the means by which the alpha radiation transfers energy to the tissue. Ionisation involves electrons being torn from the atoms of the absorbing material.
   (ii) Alpha radiation has a short range. Its effect will be more localised than that of beta radiation which has a longer range. The alpha radiation will therefore cause less harm to the healthy tissue surrounding the tumor.
   (e) Sievert

5. *(a)*

P	Q	R	S
0	1	1	1
1	1	1	0

   (b) The output switches continuously from high to low to high to low and so on in time with the input from the pulse generator. This happens because Z is an AND gate. An AND gate gives a high output when both inputs to the gate are high.
   (c) (i) Low   (ii) 2.2 V

6. *(a)* 2.1×10^6 J
   (b) (i) The value for specific latent heat of vaporisation is calculated from the ratio $\dfrac{E_h}{m}$.

   i.e. $\dfrac{\text{heat supplied}}{\text{mass of liquid vaporised}}$. Because of splashing, the mass of liquid m which is measured is bigger than that which would occur due to actual vaporisation. Because m is bigger, this means that the ratio $\dfrac{E_h}{m}$ will be smaller than that which would be obtained entirely as a result of vaporisation. Hence the measured value is less than the actual value.

   (ii) Use a container with higher sides which will prevent the splashes escaping.

7. (a) 13·2 m/s (b) 1375 N (c) 300 N
   (d) The roof rack causes a larger drag force on the car at a given speed. Therefore more work has to be done against air friction and so more fuel is consumed.

8. (a) (i) 10 V (ii) 5000 Ω (b) 2·8 °C
   (c) As the temperature decreases, the resistance of the thermistor increases. The voltage across the thermistor therefore increases. When this voltage reaches a value high enough, the transistor is switched on and the lamp lights, thereby warning the driver that the outside air temperature is dropping.

9. (a) 5625 J (b) 15 m/s (c) (i) 108 m (ii) 18·75 N

10. (a) (i) 4·2 A (ii) 25·2 A (iii) 1·26 A
    (b) Some energy is transferred as heat in the core and the coils.

11. (a) (i) $2·1 \times 10^7$ N (ii) 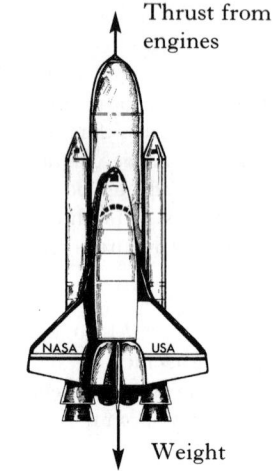
    (iii) There are no forces acting on the spacecraft and so it moves in accordance with Newton's First Law.
    (b) (i) The height would have to increase.
    (ii) 1·8 kW
    (c) (i) 1033 J/kg °C
    (ii) Silica.

12. (a) (i) 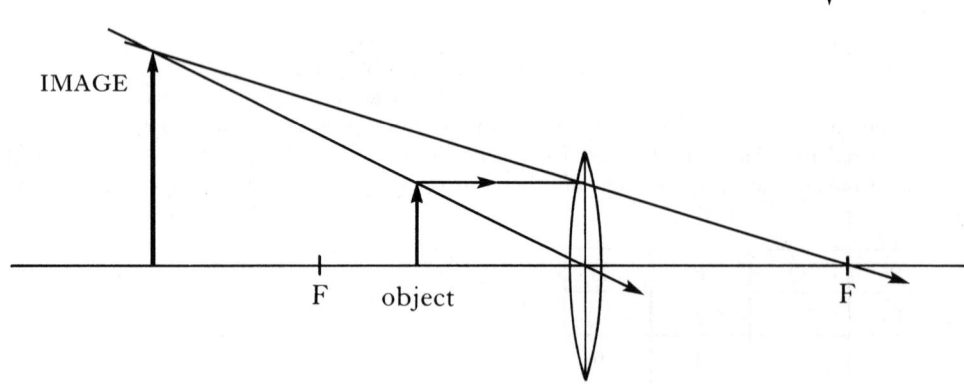
    (ii) Increase the size of the diameter of the objective lens.
    (b) (i) 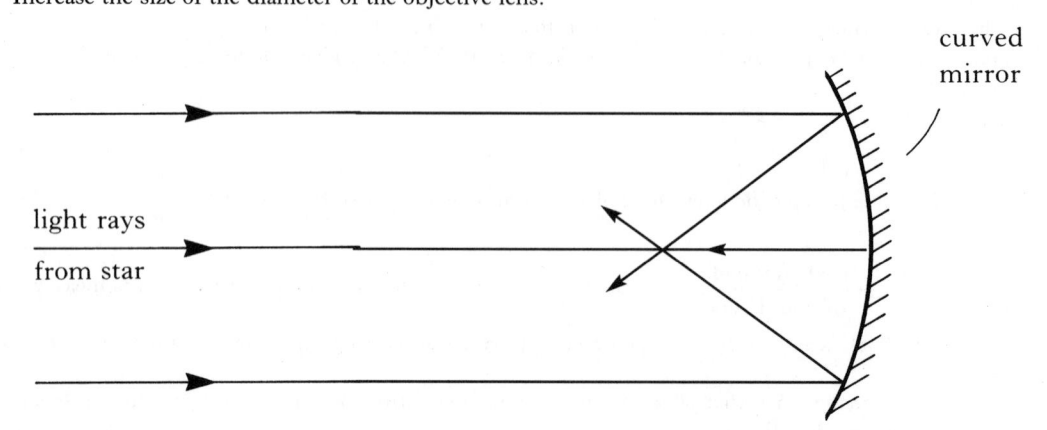
    (ii) Photographic film.
    (iii) Hydrogen and sodium.

CREDIT PHYSICS ANSWERS — 1995

1. *(a)* (i) 800 kHz (ii) 375 m
 (b) (i) (ii) 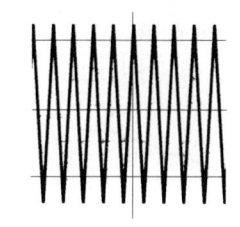 (iii) 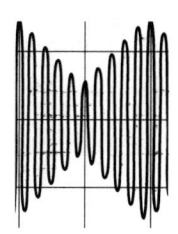
 (c) Long wave. They diffract more.

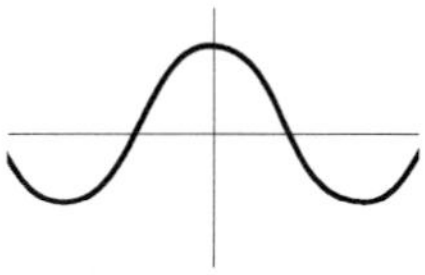

2. *(a)* (i) When one lamp fails the others stay lit. (ii) 225 Ω
 (b) Thinner wire may be used. *(c)* It can be reset.

3. *(a)* (i) (A) R (B) 1. Double insulated. No need for earth. 2. Power requires 13 A fuse.
 (ii) 48 Ω
 (iii)

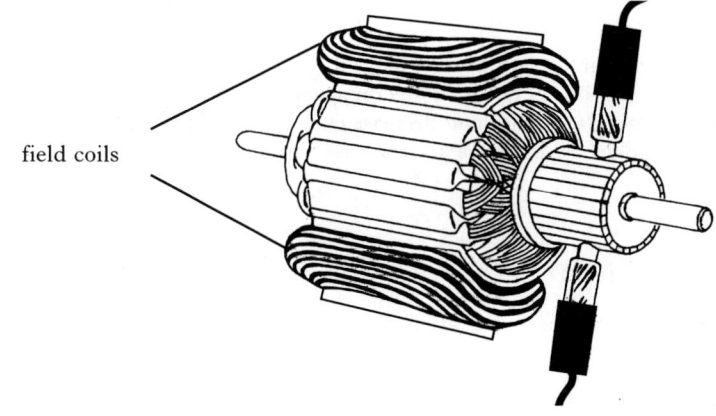

field coils

 (b) (i) Permanent magnets. (ii) Current flowing in opposite directions.
 (iii) Forces acting on coil make it rotate to a vertical position where commutator loses contact with brushes. Coil then rotates freely. Contact with brushes is again made and forces act to rotate coil.

4. *(a)* Right. More radiation is still present in kidney. *(b)* Y
 (c) 1. Too easily stopped by body tissue. 2. Causes ionisation — harmful to cells.

5. *(a)* (i) Rotation ensures all parts of cancerous tissue are treated and no one area of healthy tissue receives too much radiation.
 (ii) To avoid damage to other healthy tissue.
 (b) (i) θ_4 (ii) The normal line.

6. *(a)* 80 *(b)* 100 Hz

7. *(a)* (i) 0·5 V (ii) 4·5 V
 (b) (i) Decreases (ii) V_2 decreases, V_1 increases.
 (iii) As V_1 increases it reaches 0·7 V which switches on the transistor and lights the LED.

8. *(a)* OR gate *(b)* Z — 1 — 1 — 0 — 1
 (c) The porch lamp will always go on at night even if master is off. *(d)* Change OR gate to AND gate.

9. *(a)* 5·04 km hr^{-1} *(b)* Smaller. Part of each step is being remeasured in the next step.
 (c) Measure a step from back of one heel to back of another.

10. *(a)* (i) 8 seconds (ii) 402·5 m (iii) 5 m s⁻² (iv) 1900 N
   (b) (i) 1. When a competitor jumps in, the mass of the vehicle increases.
        2. The unbalanced force accelerating vehicle decreases.
        Since $a = \dfrac{F}{m}$ then acceleration will decrease.

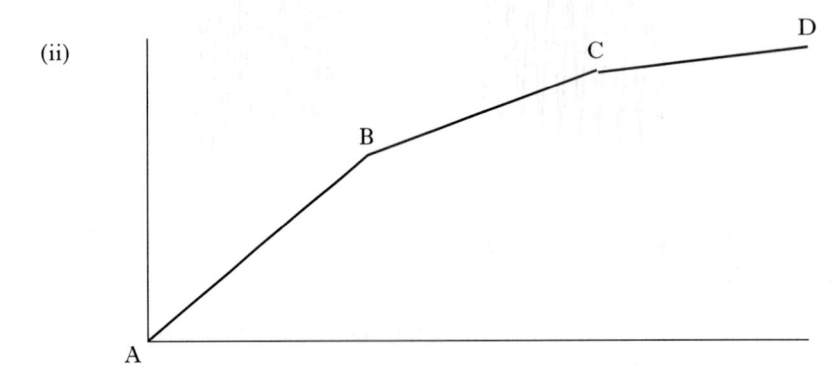

   (ii)

11. *(a)* (i) A moving magnet near a coil will induce a voltage in the coil.
        (ii) 1. Use more turns of wire in the coil. 2. Use a stronger magnet.
   (b) (i) X = step up transformer. To increase voltage and decrease current for transmission.
        Y = step down transformer. To decrease voltage and increase current.
        (ii) 8×10^6 W

12. *(a)* 511 465 J   *(b)* 1574 W
   (c) (i) The kettle also 'boils' some water which uses energy from the kettle but does not form part of Marion's calculation.
        (ii) Switch off the kettle before the water boils, e.g. at 90 °C and use a digital thermometer to record temperature.
   (d) 226 000 J

13. *(a)* (i) Makes image smaller and duller.
        (ii)

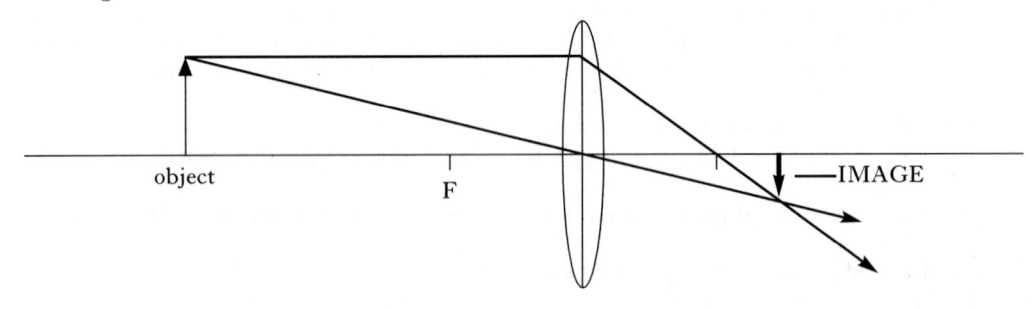

   (b) (i) P = ultra violet; Q = infra red   (ii) $f = 1 \times 10^6$ Hz Radio — TV
   (c) With reflector aimed at star, the large surface area collects a lot of radio waves. Concave shape of reflector brings waves to a focus at detector giving a strong signal.

14. *(a)* 49×10^8 J
   (b) As the meteor hits the atmosphere, friction causes it to heat up and emit light.

CREDIT PHYSICS ANSWERS — 1996

1. (a) (i) The orbit of the satellite is such that it is always positioned above the same point of the Earth's surface.
       (ii) 0·025 m.
   (b) 0·04 s.

2. (a) Thermistor (or thermocouple or photodiode ...).   (b) Tuner.
   (c) The current in the tube is increased — more electrons strike the screen every second.
   (d) (i) Red, green and blue.   (ii) Red and green.
   (e) Different shades of yellow are produced by having different brightness for the red and green dots. Different brightness of dots is produced by changing the number of electrons striking the dots every second.

3. (a) (i) Sidelights.   (ii) None.
   (b) (i) 5·17 A.
       (ii) A headlight delivers more power than a sidelight. The headlights and sidelights in a car have the same operating voltage. Therefore a headlight draws more current from the battery than a sidelight. Since a headlight draws more current it must have a smaller resistance.
   (c) Complete the diagram as follows:
       One end of Z is connected to D, the other end of Z is connected to C.

4. (a) In figure 2 the force should be drawn acting vertically downwards; in figure 3 the force should be drawn acting vertically upwards.
   (b) (i) Mark figure 4 as follows:
           (A) The electron current is shown in the direction WXYZ round the coil.
           (B) The force on WX is drawn acting vertically upwards. The force on YZ is drawn acting vertically downwards.
           (C) When viewed along the direction from P to Q, the coil rotates in a clockwise direction.
       (ii) The brushes make contact with the commutator and allow current to be supplied to the coil. As the coil rotates the commutator allows the current in the coil to change direction every half rotation, i.e. from WXYZ to ZYXW. The change in the direction of the current in the coil causes the forces acting on WX and YZ to change direction every half rotation. Thus the direction of the forces on the coil are such that they always keep the coil rotating in the same direction.
   (c) (i) Allows for smoother rotation.   (ii) Allows for operation using alternating current.

5. (a) (i) The receiver should be shown to the left of the knee on the diagram.
       (ii) The receiver is positioned to detect ultrasound reflected from the knee.
       (iii) 300 s.
   (b) (i) 20 kHz.   (ii) 1500 m/s.   (iii) Absorbed.

6. (a) The source was emitting alpha radiation since the reading was reduced when a thickness of paper was used. Gamma radiation would penetrate a block of lead 2 cm thick. The suggestion that the source is emitting alpha and gamma radiation only is therefore not correct.
   (b) Do not touch the source, use a handling tool.
   (c) (i) The effect of background radiation on the count rate has not been taken into account.
       (ii) Subtract the background count from each reading. Plot a graph of count rate against time. From the graph obtain the time taken for the count rate to reduce by half. This value represents the half-life of the radioactive source.
   (d) 50 kBq.

7. (a) (i) The hands reduce the intensity of light at the LDR. The resistance of the LDR increases. The voltage at the base of the transistor increases. When this voltage exceeds a certain value (0·6 V) the transistor is switched on and starts to conduct. A current is produced in the relay. The relay closes S_1.
       (ii) 2·5 V.
   (b) The diagram should be completed to show a capacitor connected between P and Q.

8. (a) (i) OR.
(ii) AND.
(iii)
Output 1	Output 2
0	0
1	0
1	0
1	1

(b) (i) Output 1 represents vehicles which pass over loop X or loop Y. Output 2 represents only those vehicles which pass over X and Y at the same time. Hence more pulses are detected from Output 1.
(ii) Twice.
(iii) 8.
(c) 220 Ω

9. (a) (i) 1·05 m/s^2.
(ii) 500 m.
(b) (i) (A) The pushing force is greater than air friction.
(B) The pushing force is the same size as the air friction force.
(ii) By skating in a crouching position and wearing tight fitting clothing.

10. (a) 1200 J.
(b) 48 W.

11. (a) Heat is something which flows from a hot to a cold body — a form of energy. Temperature is a measure of hotness.
(b) (i) Foam is a good insulator and so heat loss by conduction is reduced.
(ii) A shiny casing reduces heat loss by radiation.
(c) 313·5 s.
(d) The mass which now has to be heated includes a bottle and milk. More energy has to be supplied to heat this additional mass and so the time is longer.

12. (a) (i) 1·98 kW.
(ii) S.
(b) 550.
(c) (i) 75%.
(ii) Some energy is transferred as heat in the coils and core of the transformer.

13. (a) The upwards force on the diagram should be labelled "Thrust" and the downwards force should be labelled "Weight".
(b) The thrust is greater than the weight and so there is an unbalanced force in the upwards direction.
(c) 41·67 km/h/s.
(d) 132·8 N.
(e) The friction force between the spacecraft and the atmosphere on re-entry causes heat to be produced.

CREDIT PHYSICS ANSWERS — 1997

1. (a) $v = f\lambda$

   $f = \dfrac{v}{\lambda}$

   $= \dfrac{3 \times 10^8}{1190} = 252$ kHz

   This frequency is in the range 150 kHz to 270 kHz and so the radio is tuned to the LW band.

   (b) (i) The FM band is not received. The waves in this band have the shortest wavelength and do not diffract into the valley.

   (ii) The signals from the local TV station do not diffract around the hill sufficiently to reach the receiving aerial. Satellite transmissions can travel directly from the satellite to the receiving aerial.

2. (a) 1. less costly   2. many signals can be transmitted simultaneously.

   (b) The speed of the signal in copper is greater than that in glass and so the time for the copper wire system is shorter.

   (c) (i) 4·0 Hz   (ii) 0·25 V

3. (a)

Motor	Lamp L_1	Lamp L_2
off	off	off
off	on	on
on	off	off
on	on	on

   (b) $P = VI$

   $60 = 230 I$

   $I = \dfrac{60}{230}$ A

   $R = \dfrac{V}{I}$

   $= 230 \times \dfrac{230}{60} = 882$ ohms

   (c) 210 ohms

4. (a) alternating   (b) 4 V   (c) Peak voltage is greater

5. (a) Resistance when current is 0·2 A is $\dfrac{V}{I} = \dfrac{0·2}{0·2} = 1$ ohm

   Resistance when current is 1·8 A is $\dfrac{V}{I} = \dfrac{12}{1·8} = 6·67$ ohms

   Resistance increases as current increases.

   (b) At 12 V the current is 1·8 A. Power of lamp is $12 \times 1·8 = 21·6$ W.
   Power of lamp is less than that quoted by the manufacturer.

6. (a) (i)   (ii) 0·017 m

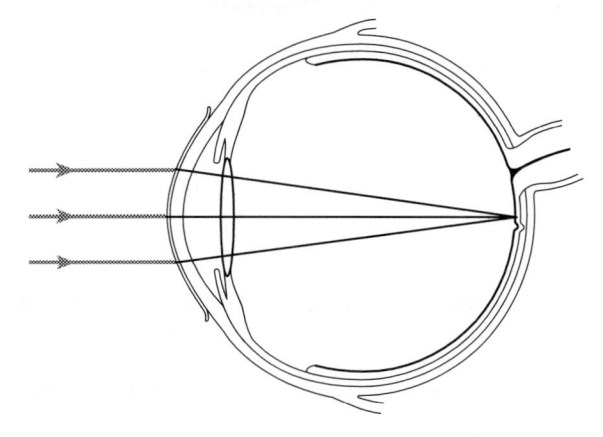

   (b) (i) The bulb is not a distant object. It is close to the lens and so the rays of light at the lens are not parellel.

   (ii) She should use an object which is a large distance from the lens.

   (c)

Lens part	Power
X	+4 D
Y	+2 D

7. *(a)* (i) Half-life is the time taken for half of the original number of radioactive atoms to decay.
   (ii) The patient is exposed to a high level of activity for as short a time as possible.
   (iii) 600 MBq to 75 MBq represents 3 half-lifes.
   3 half-lifes = 18 hours
   Sample will be ready for disposal at 7.00 am on 16/5/97.
   (b) (1) energy of radiation   (2) type of radiation.
   (c) (i) The radiation is gamma and so all the windows on the diagram should be shaded.
   (ii) The degree of "blackening" of the film is an indication of the exposure received.

8. *(a)* 0·45 V
   (b) When the package comes between the light source and the LDR the light level at the LDR decreases and its resistance increases. The voltage across the LDR increases and the voltage across the 1000 ohm resistor decreases. The voltage at the base of the resistor is reduced and the transistor switches off. The current in the coil of the electromagnet is decreased and the iron no longer makes contact with the core of the electromagnet. The switch contacts are opened, there is no current in the motor and the motor driving the conveyor belt stops.

9. *(a)*

Logic level at X	Logic level at Y
1	0
0	1

   (b) 1 Hz
   (c) Reduce the value of either C or R. This will reduce the charging and discharging time of the capacitor and so the frequency of the pulses will increase.

10. *(a)* (i) 30 m/s   (ii) The distance between the arrows would be less   *(b)* (i) 7·5 m/s   (ii) 162 N

11. *(a)* 3900 J   *(b)* (i) weight   (ii) 650 N   *(c)* 3·55 m

12. *(a)* As the bicycle wheel turns, the magnet in the dynamo rotates. The movement of the rotating magnet causes a voltage to be induced in the coil.
    (b)

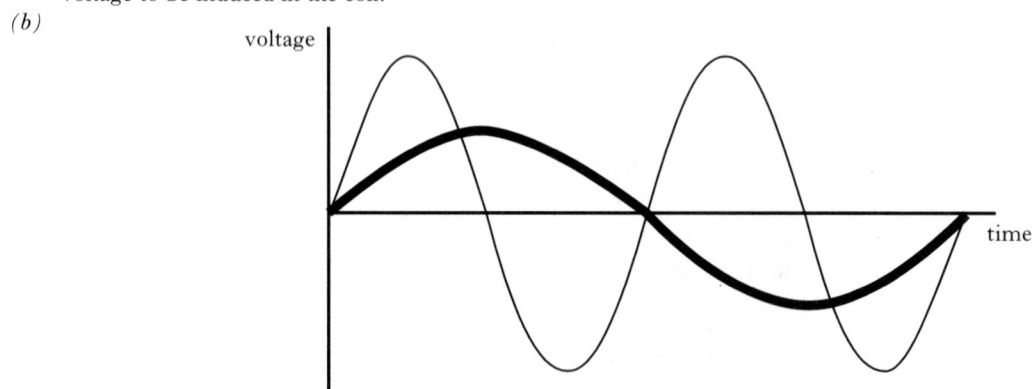

13. *(a)* (i) Liquid changes to gas.
    (ii) Heat energy is taken from the freezer compartment to produce this change of state.
    (b) $6·68 \times 10^4$ J

14. *(a)* 72   *(b)* 0·02 A
    (c) Some of the energy supplied to the primary is transferred to heat in the coils and core of the transformer.

15. *(a)* 32 000 J
    (b) The spaceship travels with a constant speed in a straight line because when the motor is switched off there is no unbalanced force acting on the spaceship.
    (c) Thruster rockets Q and S should be switched on for 10 s.

16. *(a)* The gravitational field strength on the surface of the Moon is 1·6 N/kg compared to 10 N/kg on the surface of the Earth. Hence the weight of the mirror on the Moon is less than that on Earth.
    (b) $3·84 \times 10^8$ m   *(c)* The times are equal
    (d) (i) radiation P — microwaves;   radiation Q — infrared   (ii) S

CREDIT PHYSICS ANSWERS — 1998

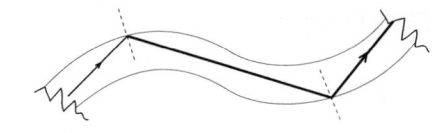

1. (a) [diagram showing light path reflecting between two mirrors]

    (b) Show working to give 0·28 s.

2. (a) (i) Infrared.
    (ii) Viewer detects maximum infrared reading when pointed towards person.
    (b) Blue and green.

3. (a) Show working to give 501 600 J.   (b) Show working to give 8360 W.
    (c) In winter water is at colder temperature so temperature rise is greater hence flow rate is less.

4. (a) When switch is closed there is a current in the coil which creates a magnetic field around the coil and attracts the iron into the coil. The moveable contact closes gap completing the circuit and motor turns.
    (b) Show working to give 1·25 m.   (c) X – commutator; Y – field coils.   (d) Show working to give 72 s.

5. (a) Show working to give 110 W.   (b) Show working to give 28·2 Ω.   (c) Show working to give 8·2 A.

6. (a) Without spectacles, light is brought to a focus in front of retina. With spectacles, light is brought to a focus on retina. Hence concave lenses.
    (b) Show working to give –1·49 dioptres.

7. (a) Q — lens absorbs UV.   (b) R — cuts down visible light.

8. (a) Time taken for half of the atoms in the source to decay.
    (b) (i) Show working to give 8 p.m.
        (ii) Lungs and thyroid, since after 8 p.m. activity is less than 200 MBq but by 2 a.m. next day activity will still be 100 MBq.

    (c)

Part of the body to be investigated	Minimum activity of solution (MBq)	Dose equivalent (SV)
Brain	800	0·0170
Lungs	80	0·0003
Liver	200	0·0027
Thyroid	40	0·0020

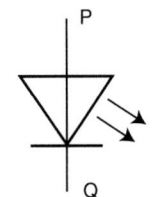

9. (a) [diagram of photodiode symbol with terminals P and Q]

    (b) (i) Show all working to give $V_1 = 0·45$ V.
        (ii) When room is dark V_1 is less than 0·7 V. Transistor is switched off.
    (c) Reverse position of LDR and 1 kΩ resistor.

10. *(a)* 4 Hz
    (b) (i) NOT gate.
    (ii) R$_2$ since the lower the value of resistance the higher the frequency of pulses.
    (c) Circuit P since with S closed voltage across 1 kΩ is 5 V.

11. *(a)* Show working to give 9 750 000 J.   *(b)* Show working to give 9 350 000 J.
    (c) Show working to give 100 m.
    (d) Vertical drop would be less since acceleration would be less due to frictional forces.
    (e) Set up light gate at S connected to computer. Measure length of vehicle. Time to cut light gate is noted.
    $$\text{Speed} = \frac{\text{length vehicle}}{\text{time to cut light gate}}.$$

12. *(a)* Reaction time is the same and speed is the same. Distance = speed × time.
    (b) Show working to give −3·3 m/s^2 *(c)* Show working to give 4950 N.
    (d) $F = ma$ hence with greater mass deceleration is reduced.

13. *(a)* In winter, greater average wind speed makes wind generator effective.
    In summer, greater average daily sunshine makes solar generator effective.
    (b) Transformers work on a.c.   *(c)* Show working to give 4600.
    (d) Transformer steps down current in line Y and power loss is given by I^2R so less current gives less power loss.

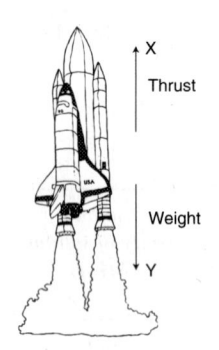

14. *(a)* (i)
    (ii) Show working to give 2·05 × 10^7 N.
    (iii) Show working to give 4·2 m/s^2.
    (b) (i) Satellite has horizontal speed.
    (ii) There is a force towards the cente of the earth.

15. *(a)* (i) Force per unit mass.   (ii) 1·6 m/s^2.
    (b) (i) Show working to give 12·5 m/s.   (ii) Show working to give 3·2 m/s.
    (iii) Distance would be less since greater field strength means time to fall is decreased.

Printed by Bell & Bain Ltd., Glasgow, Scotland.